Beyond Broadway

by
JULIAN OLNEY

DORRANCE & COMPANY • Ardmore, Pennsylvania

The flyleafs show part of a record-breaking audience of over 22,000 that greeted Andre Kostelanetz and Lily Pons in the Lewisohn Stadium, New York City, on July 17, 1939. The occasion was their first public appearance after their marriage, and the orchestra was the New York Philharmonic.

This book was inspired
by
DOROTHY MCGRAYNE OLNEY

---

*Known as Mrs. Julian Olney, she was an accomplished
presenter, manager, and producer in the performing arts.*

Ann —

May this book of my

father's exciting professional

life bring back memories.

Leslie Olney Goodale

Contents

Part Two – The Next Twenty Years

ILLUSTRATIONS

These illustrations, printed as a separate section, will be found on pages 118–135:

Introduction

Dorothy and Julian Olney first met in the fall of 1921 as comanagers of a stage show at Columbia University. He was a senior in Columbia College, and she was a senior in Barnard College, located on the other side of Broadway and 116th Street in New York City.

It had long been a tradition of the Philolexian Society to present annually an Elizabethan play. After being named manager, Olney promptly sought to break one feature of the tradition: he failed to understand why men should appear in women's roles, even though the custom had prevailed in Shakespeare's time three centuries before. He, therefore, went to Dean Virginia C. Gildersleeve and obtained permission for the girls of Barnard College to participate.

The great Shakespearian actor and coach, Louis Calvert, was secured for director. In attending the audition in the Brinkerhoff Theatre, Olney met Dorothy McGrayne of Barnard's Wigs and Cues Society for the first time. She had been named comanager by Dean Gildersleeve. Thus began a memorable lifetime collaboration.

It was twenty years later that Benjamin Welles wrote in the *New York Times:*

> Way back in 1921 Julian Olney recalls that he managed a joint Columbia-Barnard presentation of *As You Like It.* The play itself did little to enhance the reputation of William Shakespeare, but the occasion was memorable for Olney because he married the comanager from Barnard. He remembers how impressed he was with her business ability and how he took his courage in his hands when he proposed.

ix

Mrs. Olney still says: "We were married soon after the play and we've been selling tickets ever since."

Small, with large brown eyes and a broad, capable face, Mrs. Olney has spent the better part of her life managing artists, musicians and stage-folk and at the very beginning she decided that nothing was worth getting worked up about. Together with her husband Julian, . . . she has become known as a hard-working and canny judge of entertainment values.

The Olneys have staged concert series, music festivals, recitals, children's shows, dramas, musicals and other forms of entertainment. . . . They have not only learned the knack of handling artistic temperament but, moreover, they have learned how to avoid it completely themselves. So you find Mrs. Olney, busy as a bird dog, . . . moving serenely and quite unflustered by the arrival or departure of the American stage's biggest names.

Whether working jointly on some stage presentation or on separate projects (during the several years Dorothy was producer for the Ridgeway Theatre, Julian was manager of the Lewisohn Stadium Concerts), the Olneys have served in virtually every capacity connected with the production, management, and presentation of stage attractions.

After operating for many years as successful local managers in White Plains and the Westchester area of New York State, they expanded and became regional managers—presenting their attractions in nineteen other cities of New England and the northeastern United States.

Then, removing to the West Coast in 1953, their base of operations became Hollywood, California. Before long, they had taken all of California in stride and were presenting shows and concerts in every important city (eleven altogether) from Sacramento to San Diego.

Now there was nothing left but for them to become national managers—the only husband-and-wife team ever to function as such. Each year their coast-to-coast tours have gone into new towns and cities, until their road companies have now played over three hundred communities, including all the larger cities throughout the United States and Canada.

Companies touring under the aegis of the Olneys have grossed over $30,000,000. And, at the peak of their operation, they were servicing ninety-two subscription cities (not counting the usual twenty-one prime cities). The total hard-ticket buyers in one season was in excess of 1,250,000—the largest number ever generated by one management outside of the Theatre Guild cities.

Ever selective in their choice of presentations, these have always been first-rate artistically and have usually paid off ultimately. Their activities have embraced every facet of show business. This volume may either inspire or depress those who contemplate devoting their time and talents to such a profession. But, in any case, it should not leave them under any illusions.

PROLOGUE
To Peregrine Proteus from *The Life of an Actor*

Custom demands a Prologue to a Play,
And why not to a book? to pave the way.
*   *   *   *   *   *   *   *   *   *   *   *   *   *   *
No easy task new matter to afford,
When every path has been so oft explored.
*   *   *   *   *   *   *   *   *   *   *   *   *   *   *
But, with your sanction, he aspires to hope
For entertainment — there is yet much scope.
*   *   *   *   *   *   *   *   *   *   *   *   *   *   *
A kind reception the reward we ask.
. . . if you find it worth,
Over his faults with generous candor look,
Except his errors, and *accept* His Book!

—Pierce Egan, 1825

Part One

The First Twenty Years

1

The Presenter

*"The performing arts—the surest way
of communicating with people."*
—Bob Hope (November 15, 1971)

Modern society has almost eliminated use of the term *impresario*, which was once applied to those active in putting on and presenting attractions in the field of music. It was a pompous title, anyway, and the flamboyant managers who once inspired it have all but disappeared.

The designation of "presenter" has come into usage in recent years to designate those engaged in putting on stage attractions. The various functions concerned are so overlapping that one person frequently finds himself producer, promoter, manager, and a lot of other things implied by those terms.

All this is irrespective of whether the event is a ballet, concert, dramatic show, opera, or whatever event may be presented live on stage. So, for present purposes, such a person will be termed a presenter. In this capacity he is "holding the bag," win or lose, and has the privilege, therefore, of being listed first in the official billing—sometimes a dubious honor.

What of the intrepid entrepreneur whose skill and effort brings about the confluence of artists and audiences? His function can be said to be at once the most exalting or the most dejecting of occupations; it can be exasperating beyond description in one breath, a first love all over again in the next; on rare occasions it conduces to sudden riches, but more often to a depletion of assets; in short, it is just what Noah Webster must have had in mind when he wrote of a paradox: "A proposition contrary to received opinion."

Future practitioners of what the all-unknowing public customarily regards as a glamorous profession are recruited from almost anywhere. A very few may be the result of deliberate choice, but a good many of them merely happen. Very few of them, however, have been blessed with special schooling for the purpose, although they may come prepared with a wealth of amateur experience.

The presenter must be endowed with persistence to an unusual degree as well as certain temperamental qualifications. Some presenters occur as the result of an aberrational notion that to put on theatricals, concerts, etc., is actually a lot of fun — just as glamorous as it's supposed to be. It is not easy to figure out exactly what basic characteristics managers may have in common — certainly they did not go to the same school. They are qualified mainly by the rigors of experience and the ability to survive. And, above all else, they must have a feeling for showmanship.

A showman is the rugged individualist in person — and for plenty of good reasons, as will be seen later on. As a class not only are they well set apart from other fields of activity, they are all different in their own class. In fact, they are the most difficult humans in the world to bring together on any proposition, even for their own well-being. From a union standpoint, the field can be said to be overorganized; but producers, managers, and presenters are still lacking in effective organization on a national scale.

Although their problems are basically similar, the inherent nature of the business is such that no established manager seems willing to disclose in open meeting those things most vital to his own operation. Each one always thinks he has something very special on the ball; but in the aggregate, the rules and regulations relating to his work, no matter where he is located geographically, simmer down to a common denominator.

There are several different kinds of managers. The field had to become more specialized and involved to keep abreast of the modern tempo. Like the medical profession, however, the degree of specialization depends greatly on the size and location of metropolitan centers. We have our general practitioners – the country doctors who must be all things to some people all the time. These managers have to be just as resourceful and industrious, but probably have a lot more fun for their long hours.

Active in the world's greatest entertainment center, over the years Dorothy and I have undertaken almost every type of management as well as production. And that means concert manager, artist manager and booker, company manager, stock company producer, road manager, program director, Broadway coproducer, movie theater exhibitor, movie producer, lecture manager, tour bookers, national manager, etc. We have presented on stage all types of worthwhile attractions for which tickets of admission could be sold.

So much depends on mere human judgment that even experience cannot always provide the right answers. As one manager was heard to remark, "I don't trust anyone's judgment but my own, and mine is not to be relied on." This may be a reason why show business is on occasion considered a hit-or-miss business. For success, it does require an exact knowledge based on a fund of experience and a high degree of skill as well. And it does need something else – still more important – a flair for showmanship.

In writing on the presentation of stage attractions to audiences, which we believe deserves to be denoted a profession by now, much personal experience has been drawn upon. As associates, we have handled and presented a long roster of attractions, including many "names," so, naturally, some have become drawn into this discussion. For the most part they will appear in a favorable light, in a few instances, not so favorable. In the latter case it cannot be helped – such was the experience.

While this is largely a resumé of personal experience, it is intended to serve primarily as background for a bird's eye view of the whole fascinating field of stage entertainment beyond the confines of Broadway.

To the uninitiated it may be glamorous, but as for the presenter – he is far more interested in what is left over in the settlement than in any nebulous prestige the affair may have

5

gained for him. With these few preliminaries, let us consider the stage set for the presentation of *Beyond Broadway*. Many years of experience, including the usual heartbreaks as well as the occasional triumphs, have gone into making this particular production. The process has been thrilling and eminently worthwhile. For—let no one be deceived—the entertainment game, particularly under the impetus of modern invention, has now become one of the world's essential industries. The evolution from art to industry is dealt with subsequently.

In these times the performing arts have become just about as necessary as food and drink, or clothes and shelter. Never before did show business flourish as during the late war. And never before was such a gigantic effort expended to provide live entertainment for the troops on global battlefronts. For this purpose the USO raised and expended millions of dollars. And this, in spite of the prevalence of movies and radio, which were never heard on a battlefield in World War I.

Until quite recently a restricted field of human effort considered dispensable, entertainment has become indispensable. And in spite of the so-called entertainment being purveyed daily to countless millions by mechanical contrivances, the comparatively slim ranks of the legitimate theatergoers, the concert lovers, and the balletomanes have managed to maintain their formations. It is to be hoped that the performing arts have not suffered too much from mechanical intrusion but rather that the mass media have added to their devotees.

All of this helps to explain why we feel that the entrepreneur, producer, or manager of stage presentations has come to assume such an important role in modern living. So let us pull back the curtain and see if this mysterious world behind the proscenium can offer a lure to him who would hazard his hopes and future on public response at the box office.

2

The Making of a Concert Series

"The arts are ladders to heaven by which man may ascend to God."
—Abdul

A million-dollar "all-purpose" building erected with tax-payers' money to house the recreational activities of the citizens was much more a novelty in 1930 than today. Since World War II, many similar buildings are to be found from coast to coast. The impressive Westchester County Center, located on the Bronx River Parkway in White Plains, New York, was once the last word in such buildings.

To be successful, the presentation of cultural events anywhere must have sufficiently strong reasons to expect support enough from the community to pay the bills. Dedicated enthusiasm for the project on the part of the sponsor, added to the desire of the community for the attractions, will bring rewards to both. With a potential seating capacity of fifty-two hundred persons, the Westchester County Center intrigued us as an ideal place in which to present world-famous attractions; and its great stage had all the facilities necessary to accommodate the Metropolitan Opera, which it did for two seasons at the outset. Furthermore, it was ideally located in the heart of Westchester County, about twenty-five miles from New York City, with an adjacent population composed largely of persons having above-average incomes.

In seeking local sponsorship, several organizations asked the Olneys to manage presentations for them. These included moving pictures by Williamson, the noted underseas photographer; a series of remarkable professional plays for children produced by Adrienne Morrison (the mother of Joan, Barbara, and Constance Bennett); a dance recital by Angna Enters; and finally a concert by Seth Parker, of radio fame.

These experiences, plus past personal interest in everything "on stage in person," prompted us to contact several bureaus in New York City to learn who and what was available, as well as playing time and terms. Fred Schang, of Columbia Concerts Corporation, was helpful from the beginning and, along with Sol Hurok, became our mentor and adviser. Thus began a long and fascinating association with artists and audiences.

The Westchester County Center was under the direction of a Recreation Commission, which consisted of five prominent, public-spirited women, headed by Mrs. Eugene Meyer. They inaugurated and supervised a balanced program of cultural events of high caliber. As long as Mrs. Meyer remained the inspired chairman of this group, the center was well run and attracted outstanding events. Her removal to Washington, D. C., however, proved a deterrent to continuation of this high-minded policy.

It was with their encouragement that we proceeded to book those events which might appeal to a Westchester audience. At the end of our first season we were surprised to find we had lived through the presentation of thirteen major attractions plus a second season of Adrienne Morrison's Children's Players. There was no profit, but the experience acquired was abundant.

The first major presentation (1931) was the famed Ruth St. Denis with a large company of dancers. The program featured mainly those colorful, interpretive dances of the Far East on which her vast reputation had been made. According to the New York *Herald-Tribune*, "it was seen to distinct advantage," and "her pictorial and resourceful dance of Salome shared the honors with her glittering Balinese dance and her modern

Nautch dance." This remarkable artist thirty years later was still presenting dance programs in person with her students in Hollywood.

On several occasions we were guests at Denishawn House, the exotic home Ruth and her husband, Ted Shawn, had built in the Bronx section of New York City. She always expected her guests to enjoy sitting in Oriental fashion on cushions on the floor while she and they could at the same time observe their awkwardness in the huge mirrors all about.

Later, in the same season, Vicente Escudero and his Spanish gypsy dancers were presented. Other ensembles included the inimitable Tony Sarg Marionettes; *The Chocolate Soldier*, as presented by the New York Opera Comique; and the Don Cossack Russian Male Chorus. This last group had just enjoyed a sensational success at Carnegie Hall prior to the opening of its second American tour. It was to become a perennially popular attraction, always drawing large and enthusiastic audiences.

The dynamic young conductor, Serge Jaroff, accounted to some extent for this popularity. He had a striking ramrod-erect figure and knew how to milk the applause from a willing audience. One critic wrote, "The concert given—entirely unaccompanied with no guide but the leader's pitchpipe—was unlike anything ever heard here before. The majority may have been soloists, but the miracle recognized was the effortless tone production that made each number a dramatic incident." No one else sings so effectively the "Song of the Volga Boatmen"—"Ay, Ookhnem."

Our first important financial success was the presentation of Mr. and Mrs. Martin Johnson with their remarkable motion pictures, accompanied by tales of adventure in Africa. So great was the interest in the Johnsons that the curtain was held for nearly half an hour to allow over fifteen hundred persons (who had not purchased their tickets in advance) to be seated. These world-famous explorers, who shot with the camera instead of the gun, thrilled the huge audience with their panorama of strange places, peoples, and animals. Mrs. Johnson, familiarly known as Osa, was a charmingly chic feminine figure in a modish black velvet gown—scarcely looking the part of a hardy jungle explorer. One of the great film–lecture attractions of

9

all time, the Johnsons made a stunning appearance and commanded a fee of $1,000 — top money for a lecture program in the early 1930s.

In our first season we brought to Westchester audiences several other artists who had been dominant figures for many years. One of these was Mischa Elman, who had made his debut in 1908. Many years later, his fiftieth anniversary was to be celebrated while he was still giving concerts in top form as a major recitalist. Just before going out on the stage, the familiar Elman ceremony was enacted when six members of the family, including father Elman, lined up so that each could embrace in turn their talented Mischa. The father had been always a great help and inspiration in encouraging his son's remarkable career.

Except for the lecture by Winston Churchill, which will be covered in a special chapter, the most important and unusual event of this first season was the joint concert of Paul Robeson and the Hall Johnson Choir. Of this performance Henry Beckett of the New York *Evening Post*, wrote:

> There took place at the Westchester County Center in White Plains last night an event of consequence in the history of the American Negro. That is the first thing to be said about a concert which was also significant in the development of music on American soil. For the first time anywhere there was heard a program shared by a Negro, who is at least the greatest individual singer of his race, and by a choir which in our opinion is the most authentic and vital in the singing of spirituals.
>
> The soloist was Paul Robeson; the choral ensemble was the Hall Johnson Choir. Both seemed to "feel the spirit," both gave unsparingly to make the concert a superb demonstration of the Negro's art in song. The audience of thousands realized this and knew that the advance notice was not an exaggeration! "A double attraction without parallel in the concert annals of Westchester or elsewhere," it said, and that is what the concert was.

The reception given to the various events in the first season left no doubt that for the next year a series of attractions would be offered on a subscription basis to give the project more stability. Those in the county who heretofore had had to be content to read about world-famous artists would now find them readily accessible in their midst. Fortunately, the

Westchester County Center's capacity was such that it was possible to have one thousand seats at $1.65 and several hundred at $1.10 for student groups. Thus the events reached all brackets of income.

It so happened that we had entered the concert arena near the end of a period of giants, the like of which do not exist today. Although we just missed out on Amelita Galli-Curci, Enrico Caruso, Ernestine Schumann-Heink, Jean and Édouard de Reszke, and others, we were able to offer comparable artists, as will be noted shortly.

Fritz Kreisler, celebrated beyond most artists of the musical world, was booked for the opening of this first subscription season. By special arrangement with Mrs. Eugene Meyer, Chairman of the County Recreation Commission, the entire net proceeds of the sold-out house (with one hundred standees) was devoted to musical activities sponsored by the commission. The five other events included Chaliapin, the Vienna Boys' Choir, the Don Cossacks (repeated), Percy Grainger, and Rosa Ponselle.

The first check for box seats was received from the farsighted county political leader, William L. Ward, who never failed to back artistic and cultural improvements in the area for which he had done so much. Boxes seating six were purchased by other prominent county residents, and attendance came from more than thirty surrounding communities. At each concert the charming hostesses in evening dresses passed out the programs, for which they earned money for the junior division of the White Plains Woman's Club.

Rosa Ponselle purchased the first two subscriptions to be given away to music students of exceptional promise. Along with other gifts, such concert awards covered ten high schools, a policy that continued for the next fifteen years.

In order that all those interested might be reached, a capable and charming woman from each of sixteen communities was selected to personally contact the music lovers of her city by phone, mail, or in person and so offer them the opportunity to enjoy the privileges presented by this new subscription series. Prominent in this group was Mrs. Harold Bennett of Scarsdale, a most enthusiastic supporter and loyal friend of music. When she first started telephoning, the question was asked "Is this a

11

benefit?" Her prompt reply was, "Yes, indeed, a benefit to you."

The first major financial disappointment came with the concert by Rosa Ponselle. Then at the height of her career at the Metropolitan Opera, she was considered the outstanding dramatic soprano of her day. Although a superb recitalist, she drew the same-sized audience as the Vienna Boys' Choir, but her fee was two and one-half times as much!

As in all branches of show business, there is always a ready alibi for box-office ailments, and the current one for this concert was that Italians go to hear their singers only in opera—not in concert! Even with the knowledge, however, that the audience had paid in only enough to cover Miss Ponselle's fee (other expenses amounting to $1,500 represented the deficit), we still could agree with the review that "it was a recital matchless in beauty, incomparable in artistic perfection." Not only did she have the gift of song, but her appearance in a ravishing fur-trimmed, white satin gown "sold" her to the audience on her first entrance.

Mrs. Fritz Kreisler was said to be in good measure responsible for Mr. Kreisler's great success, as he was inclined to be lazy when left to himself. It was she who always took charge of proceedings backstage. When he finally started the concert, however, she would disappear completely and was once discovered in a dressing room deeply immersed in a mystery book called *Black Magic*. Always lovable and gracious, Mr. Kreisler was popular with the public and appeared for us in several successive concerts.

The chief financial advantage of selling concerts on a subscription basis rather than as single events was, of course, that a couple of less-expensive programs could be part of a season package and help to level the costs of the name artists needed to sell the series. Also, the occasional loss can be more readily absorbed.

By now we had become accustomed to all the facets of promotion. These included advance publicity—news stories, pictures, interviews, social notes to ten daily papers, twenty-four weeklies (eight Connecticut papers and five in New York City); mailing special letters and information for group sales and announcements to twenty public school music supervisors, fourteen women's club magazines, thirty libraries, ninty-nine church groups, twenty-five nursing homes, twenty-seven drama clubs, seventeen private schools and colleges, sixty-three high schools, nineteen YW and YMCAs, and twenty-one music stores; servicing sixteen representatives; arranging for the distribution of several hundred window cards and the posting of a few dozen three sheets (those attractive color poster sheets one sees on buildings — 40" x 60").

There are always those seeking to entertain an artist with a party after a concert. It is not easy to explain how difficult it is usually for an artist to accept. Touring is exhausting enough, not to mention the evening's performance; and probably there is a concert to follow on the next night. Since the manager does not leave the building until all the public has left and until after they have returned for lost articles or to use the telephone when the car will not start, he arrives exhausted at a party of his own friends. After a quick cup of coffee to keep awake, he then goes home to toss something up in his own kitchen and to tell the family that there must be an easier way to make a living. But the next day the telephone rings with gratifying remarks from subscribers who have enjoyed a memorable evening. Then after an appreciative review comes out in the evening paper, the manager is ready to start promoting the next attraction.

Feodor Chaliapin, the great Russian basso who had made his debut forty years before, was one of the most colorful and exciting performers of all time. When the advance program arrived, it was, of course, printed up in full for the program. Two days before the concert an entirely new program arrived to everyone's dismay. This was mimeographed and inserted in the printed program. No one should have been concerned, however, for he had no intention of following a formal program in any event. Instead, he went out on stage carrying a pile of music, which he plunked down on the piano and from which he selected numbers at random as the spirit moved him. When he found the house in darkness at the outset, he ordered the house lights to be put up. To the audience he explained that everything should look gay. It was his magnetic personality plus vocal art and an extraordinary acting talent that sustained his unique position as an artist long after his voice had passed its prime.

13

Feodor Chaliapin, after his concert in 1932, drew a cartoon of himself and inscribed his autobiography "To charming Madame Julian Olney."

He was a giant in his time, nor has his like been seen since.

One of the devices used to make the public conscious of the consistent high quality of the concert events presented and to give them unity as a continuing series was personal presentation of each artist to the audience. Mrs. Julian Olney's remarks were limited to a few sentences, which most of the artists appreciated. It also served a good purpose in getting the audience settled before the program began. Chaliapin's disposition, however, was reputed to be tempestuous. He had been known to throw chairs around backstage when displeased, and the management was advised to omit the introduction. But when notified of our procedure, all he did was throw kisses to Dorothy; then after she left the stage he strode on stage and went into the first number with gusto. She was sent his autobiography later with a delightful self-portrait drawn on the flyleaf of his book, *Pages from My Life,* and inscribed to "charming Madame Julian Olney."

It is always interesting to watch audience reaction to the touches of showmanship employed by some artists that help to put over their programs. These may be found in the choice and arrangement of the program itself, style of the costume, personality, or in the method of staging the performance. Such items customarily receive a good going-over during the intermission chitchat.

The Vienna Boys' Choir inevitably enchanted their audiences from the outset. A review in the White Plains *Daily Reporter* commented, "The lights dimmed, the footlights went up, and through the velvet curtains stepped twenty-one small boys, each dressed sailor fashion in dark trousers and white blouses. At a chord from their director, they began singing, the flutelike voices opening up with "Oh, say can you see." The large audience rose and stood while these small visitors continued with our national anthem, their quaint accent adding charm to familiar words. By the time the last note had been sung, the Wiener Saengerknaben had completely won the hearts of everyone. The evening was justly theirs." It is small wonder that the attraction has continued to concertize so successfully for well over four decades throughout America.

Not to be overlooked for junior audiences was the enchanting Tony Sarg Marionettes—always a hit with the youngsters year

15

after year. And, in concerts, no programs were ever selected with more care and executed with greater finesse than Thomas Scherman's Concerts for Young People. It was a pleasure to present them each season.

After the first ten years, more or less, we began to be confronted with the awful thought that we could not possibly put together a suitable series for the following year. Having survived the early birth pains, this consideration was a recurring problem by January of every year. It had been the policy at the last event of each season to announce the events for the succeeding season. It brought in many renewals before the summer months introduced other interests.

Many contingencies always had to be taken into account. The series had to contain some name artists but not too many for the budget; there must be a strong opening and closing; the dates available at the auditorium had to conform to those open on the artists' schedules; the attractions should be secured from different bureaus; repetition of a concert sooner than after a year's lapse was usually inadvisable; and, above all, there must be a balanced variety of events.

3

Heyday of the Olney Series

*"The real artist has no pride at all;
he knows, alas, that art has no limits;
he senses daily how far distant he is
from the goal."*
—*Beethoven*

One of the more lucid writers on various aspects of music was Olin Downes, music critic of the *New York Times*. In an essay entitled "The Future of the Recital," he once wrote that "certain musicians continue to command a public; and the public, despite hard times, has shown that when convinced of the attractiveness of a musical performance, will patronize it. . . . What music needs and what concerts need is simply presentation which has vitality and significance."

This was precisely the goal for which we strove in our method of presentation. With the selection of an attractive series always uppermost, an advisory committee was formed early to meet for discussion and reaction regarding the tastes of the public. The committee was made up of a dentist, a lawyer, a president of a national company, a women's club president, two musicians, and a writer. For a number of years this group met to mutual advantage for the airing of problems, and the resultant enthusiasms made for progress.

Another step taken was the establishment of a group of

17

subscribing patrons. Originally they were backers, to the extent of one hundred dollars each. Their attendance and patronage was of help because of the publicity involved and the wideness of their contacts. Among these supporters were included Miss Anne Morgan, Mrs. Lewis Bloomingdale, Mr. Raymond M. Gunnison, Miss M. Elizabeth Read, Mrs. John Stillwell, Mr. William L. Ward, Mrs. Jay L. Rothschild, Mrs. C. B. Winslow, and other prominent county residents.

The list of celebrities and outstanding ensemble attractions lengthened with the years. It would serve no purpose to discuss each individually here, so a list has been included in the appendix II. This list is an almost complete roster of the more important concert and road attractions playing on tour during the 1930s and 1940s. There was a time when no new attraction felt it had made the grade until it was selected for the Olney series.

Some series shaped up better than others; but the one that included Jascha Heifetz, Lawrence Tibbett, the Hall Johnson Choir, Uday Shan Kar and Dancers, Sergei Rachmaninoff, and Lily Pons seemed to be an ideal selection. For the first time there was included a dance attraction as part of a music season, though it is not unusual to do so nowadays. Uday Shan Kar with his Hindu dancers in their gorgeous costumes, accompanied by exotic music played on fifty-six varieties of instruments, combined to produce rare enchantment. Heifetz, Tibbett, Rachmaninoff, and Pons were to be repeated through the years because of their perennial popularity.

In this first appearance of Tibbett on the Olney series, his program brought sharp criticism. Called a "miscellaneous song recital," it showed the influence of his radio programs, on which he attempted to please everyone. As an encore to Handel's glorious "Hear Me Ye Winds and Waves," he sang a cute little song—"Elegy on the Death of a Mad Dog." No purpose was served by objecting to the program in advance, as changes were refused. Perhaps the greatest of American singing actors, Tibbett's subsequent programs were always a glorious experience.

Although Rachmaninoff's programs were always a joy to his

audiences in every number, they were never satisfied to leave until he had played his own famous Prelude in C-sharp minor. Backstage he would express disdain for the piece and complain about having to play it. His audiences, however, were always large and appreciative, and his checks were also of generous proportions. Rachmaninoff had one special reason to remember his engagement at the Westchester County Center. Usually of grave countenance, he once beamed with a broad smile when commenting that the easy chair provided in his dressing room was the most comfortable chair he had ever found on any tour.

Securing a concert engagement for Lily Pons was always subject to call by the Metropolitan Opera, but her popularity negated any amount of trouble involved in getting her appearances. Not only was she the leading coloratura soprano in the world, but her petite and chic appearance, her impeccable French gown (with tiny hat and muff), and her gracious personality all served to endear her to audiences everywhere. She once told us about the charming gift of an ivory elephant from King Prajadhipok when he visited this country, to which a note had been attached saying, "You are to other singers what the elephant is to all other animals." For many years she continued to be the "queen of the coloratura range."

From the beginning, we staged all our concerts, thus giving attention to the dressing of the stage as well as to the proper conditions for hearing. We had a special acoustical stageset built and decorated exclusively for our events. It afforded an attractive background for the artist, and the colorful bouquets arranged on each side of the stage, the lush red velvet proscenium curtains, and blue carpeting on the aisles all conspired to make a gala setting for these concerts.

Josef Hofmann had already been concertizing on three continents for nearly half a century when first presented in the Olney series. Piano students always marvelled at the dexterity of his famous left hand. Commenting on this, he said it was "merely the means to an end, for no matter how great technique may be, if the soul be lacking, if the player has not the inborn spark, no technique, no matter how great, will make that person a great artist." In the controversy on modernistic music,

Hofmann felt that "music has no age—it is good or bad, not old or new. Let us play the best, regardless of whether it was written yesterday or three hundred years ago. But let us remember at the same time that if a thing is interesting only because it is new, it will remain interesting only as long as it is new."

In the *New York Times* of November 1937, Brooks Atkinson wrote of Josef Hofmann, "He now stands, ripened in wisdom, and with youthful power, the master who forges a beauty linking the mighty past with the living present, making us know once more that art is a thing ageless and eternal, by which man can live who cannot live by bread alone."

Through the years, we always devoted much time and effort to encouraging young people to attend the concerts. It was believed that if they learned to enjoy them early, concert going would become a pleasurable lifetime habit. Since prices had to be low, the presentation of events especially for children was a labor of love and always incurred deficits. The answer to this problem eventually came with the advent of Thomas Scherman and his Little Orchestra. He has done a remarkable job with his special concerts for children, which we sponsored in Westchester for several successive seasons.

The type of instrumentalists that seem to always have the widest audience appeal are the pianists. Perhaps they are usually a safer audience draw because so many people can identify themselves with the performer, remembering their own days of practicing and of mastering piano technique.

In the days when most recital artists had an established flat fee, several of them were inevitably overpaid in comparison with their box-office draw. In 1934 we paid José Iturbi $750 and lost money. Nine years later, after his motion-picture success, we paid him $7,093 for a concert in Newark and $6,907 for another concert in White Plains. With all the expenses to come out of the balance, the management was still left with a fair margin, after considerable risk in both cases.

A fair guarantee of an amount to be paid for services, plus a reasonable percentage of the box office after an amount allowed for the cost of putting on the concert or entertainment, is usually an ideal contract. If an artist will play only for an astronomical guarantee, then he may not be too sure of his own box-office draw.

In the course of offering hundreds of presentations, only one star performer ever asked after the event if we made out all right financially. It was Admiral Byrd, who inquired if his one-thousand-dollar fee left enough margin to the manager for his trouble. He was accustomed to figuring the costs of his own explorations.

In addition to the subscription offerings, many special attractions were presented as they became available after booking the series. Some of these are covered in detail in the chapter on special events.

In a feature story, the *Musical Courier* once touched on a problem of survival that was increasing for local impresarios each year. Eventually it became an important reason for getting out of the presentation end of the concert business. The magazine wrote, "Disapproving heartily of 'block' system buying, the Olneys have steadfastly resisted all attempts at taking away their freedom and they have remained one of the few independent series managers in the country."

In four recitals within four years by Nelson Eddy just prior to World War II, we grossed $34,000 and set a national tour record with receipts of $11,680 in one night. This being his exclusive New York metropolitan appearance at the time, the railroad ran special trains to accommodate the customers. It also held the last trains back to New York until the concerts were over!

One big problem for management was in adequately protecting Mr. Eddy. He was held in such adulation by the crowds (not only teenagers) that he could not eat in a public restaurant or send his clothes to a public laundry, and the buttons of his coat were pulled off for souvenirs. Many gifts were received for him backstage. One time a group of young ladies from an exclusive private school sent him a ring to wear during the concert so they would know that he had read their letter. He was a handsome, personable artist who enjoyed all the fuss with no conceit and much good humor.

At the close of an Eddy concert, fourteen stalwart Parkway policemen would form a line across the front of the stage so that

21

the audience could not reach him, and then they formed a guard to get him into the car at the stage door. The next day his manager told the press it had been the best managed concert of his nationwide tour. Said the Macy newspapers in the headline of their syndicated review, "Glorious Voice and Charming Personality of Idol Hold 6000 Spellbound."

Through her art and personality Marian Anderson became a beloved figure in the world of music. At the time we first presented her in the 1930s, she had sung at the White House and for the king and queen of England and had notched up an all-time record of seventy-five concerts in sixty cities in one season. She also became a national issue when use of Constitution Hall was denied to her, causing Eleanor Roosevelt to resign from the DAR and prompting the United States government to offer her the use of Lincoln Memorial for an outdoor concert in Washington.

All the regular seats were sold ten days before her performance, and again the SRO sign was put out, as it had been for Nelson Eddy. Her program covered a wide range—German Lieder, Italian arias, English songs, and a group of spirituals. Probably the favorite song of the evening was the Shubert "Ave Maria," although others might argue for "Deep River" or "Crucifixion." Kosti Vehanen, for nine years Miss Anderson's accompanist, provided excellent support. As a composer, he also contributed two charming Finnish songs to the program. Many fine accompanists were part of the concert programs, and only too often they are taken for granted.

On its advent in New York in 1932, Col. W. de Basil's Ballet Russe de Monte Carlo was hailed by the critics as the most intriguing and glamorous dance ensemble to be brought to these shores since the Diaghilev Ballet in 1917. The announcement read, "Representing the highest in theatre art, the Russian ballet, once the restricted delight of only kings and emperors, combines in its scope drama and comedy, music, painting and dancing. The company of one hundred includes a symphony orchestra." In association with S. Hurok, we had the honor to include in our series the "sensation of London, Paris, and New York" on its first American tour. The program included "Union Pacific," "Les Sylphides," and "Le Beau

Danube"—all delightful numbers. The Ballet Russe was repeated many times over the years, always to the delight of large audiences and with profit to the sponsor.

The ballet operated theoretically on a nonstar system. Once the protocol was very nearly upset when the program cover carried a picture of Tamara Toumanova. To avoid hair pulling among the prima ballerinas, fortunately Mr. Hurok made the discovery in time. So four thousand new covers carrying the picture of Colonel de Basil were printed on the day of the performance. In addition to Toumanova, this remarkable cast included Riabouchinska, Alexandra Danilova, Irina Baronova, David Lichine, and Léonide Massine.

Backstage at the ballet the smell of greasepaint is ever a familiar odor, but fish glue is not. Upon inquiry, it was found that the connection between this unexpected substance and ballet dancing is simple enough. It has to do with the elaborate rite of donning the ballet slipper, to which a ballerina gives even more time than an actress devotes to her makeup.

First the silk tights, the classic maillot, are smoothed over the foot. Then a thin film of cotton is spread across the toes, thicker for matinee days, when every crack in the stage floor is a chasm. Then the slipper goes on, and the dancer poises on her toe again and again to make sure it is right. And now at last comes the fish glue, a tiny drop of it in the heel to fix it in place. Finally, the satin ribbons are wound around the ankle and tied. Then the feet are ready.

The preparation and perspiration that go into the Ballet Russe de Monte Carlo "as it swings annually in a cloud of resin across the American continent" is unknown to the millions who flock to the box office. When the Ballet Russe "special" steamed into town, it had four baggage cars loaded with scenery, props, costumes, trunks, musical instruments, and electrical equipment, plus six sleepers loaded with seventy dancers. There were nine hampers full of shoes alone and an almost endless array of costumes!

Other interesting dance groups that had drawn good audience reactions from time to time included Shan Kar and his Indian Dancers, the Bali Dancers, Escudero, Ted Shawn and Company, and the Jooss Ballet. Kurt Jooss and his European

Ballet scored a distinct hit with their repertory of unique modern-dance numbers. A rollicking fantasy of fun and folly was "Johann Strauss, Tonight"; and the famous "Green Table" graphically portrayed the aftermath of the horrors of war.

It was not until Sol Hurok introduced the Ballet Russe de Monte Carlo to American audiences, however, that the dance could be said to have come of age in this country. Thereafter it was to grow in importance, developing an ever larger following in addition to those balletomanes who were the nucleus of the dance audience in every community. And so dance has become established as a major form of stage art in its own right. And, where the Broadway musical shows once depended on singing choruses for their ensemble work, they now use dance patterns.

4

A Twenty-Year Run Is Ended

"All entertainment is not art,
but all art is entertainment"
—Rouben Mamoulian

After a two-year hiatus during World War II, we reopened our concert series with renewed enthusiasm with the first local appearance of Artur Rubinstein. The noted Polish pianist had been traveling many thousands of miles yearly to carry his dynamic music to the more peaceful areas of the world. The event was an auspicious beginning, to be followed by a superb symphony concert.

Four thousand people attended this first local appearance of the famed Boston Symphony Orchestra. The occasion was a personal triumph for Leonard Bernstein, who was conducting. John D. Chequer wrote in the *Mount Vernon Argus*, "Here was no time-beater. Bernstein shook his fists at the orchestra, he beat time with his shoulders, he swayed his body like a ballerina, he employed his hands as vocal parts of the orchestra, and when his hands were busy bringing in one set of instruments, his head was indicating a coming entrance for another group. May the writer suggest that last night the audience of 4000 saw one of the great conductors of tomorrow, not as a neophyte, but as a full-grown artist." This was written in February of 1947.

Other notable orchestra conductors and concerts followed. Among them were the redoubtable Eugene Ormandy, conducting the Philadelphia Orchestra; and at another time Leopold Stokowski conducted the same aggregation of master musicians. On another memorable occasion Artur Rodzinski conducted the Cleveland Orchestra. The soloist was Oscar Levant, who played the Piano Concerto in F Major by George Gershwin. With Stephen Hero as violin soloist, the Rochester Philharmonic Orchestra under the baton of José Iturbi was presented.

A genuine audience charmer was the Danish Heldentenor Lauritz Melchior. Possessed of an infectious personality and equipped with superb vocal artistry, he became the ideal concert attraction when touring with his own orchestra of forty players. He had also enjoyed a distinguished career in opera houses all over the world. So when he became a hit in moving pictures, new impetus was added to an already full career. Some of his audiences went wild. At the close of the program he always invited them to join in the chorus of "Vive la Compagnie," which they did with gusto.

He was usually famished after a concert, but suitable eating places were not always open, especially on a Sunday night. On one such night we stopped at a place along the highway where Lauritz found the steak very much below par. But, like the gracious gentleman he was, when the waitress nervously asked if everything was all right, he said with a smile, "Yes, just fine, my dear." Then he put the meat in a bag in which he carried his special protein bread and took it home for the benefit of his Great Dane, who was not nearly so discriminating.

Vladimir Horowitz was another of the outstanding box-office favorites, always selling out in his later years of concertizing. The adjectives applied to him were "breathtaking," "electrifying," "inimitable piano virtuoso," etc. While these qualities may be apparent to the audiences, one cannot forget especially his meticulousness in preparing for a concert. He left the responsibility of checking on the stage arrangements and his piano to no one but came to the auditorium himself early on the afternoon of the concert. He carefully had the lights and acoustics tested. Then he rested in a dressing room before the concert, knowing that all was in readiness.

The main problem in planning season-by-season cultural events now seemed to be an increasing lack of exciting new personalities and extraordinary talent. The war had stemmed the usual influx of European artists, and it was not feasible to continue repeating artists who were no longer at their best. Then there was an obvious trend toward ensemble attractions. A novelty like the First Piano Quartet of radio fame became box office overnight; entertainment on a high level, nevertheless it had an enormous popular appeal. Occasionally popular programs were presented, such as Stan Kenton and his Orchestra, Fred Waring and his Pennsylvanians, and Spike Jones and his City Slickers.

For some time the effects of a serious new development in the music business were being felt all over the country. The scheme, now generally known as the Organized Audience Plan (or the captive audience plan), was used in setting up Community Concert Series and Civic Concert Series.

It was employed primarily by the two largest artists managements in the country, Columbia Concerts Corporation and National Concerts and Artists Corporation. It was a slick device for selling concert tickets and talent at the same time. There is no doubt that the system has extended employment in certain classes of artists. Also, it is of value to a community that is unable to support concerts in any other way. Quite simply, the concert bureau sends out a trained staff member or paid organizer to a community carefully selected in advance. He surveys the town and eventually finds a man or woman who, through love of music or a sense of civic duty or social aspirations, agrees to head up a local committee.

A one-week drive is put on to get subscribers to buy memberships at five and six dollars for four, five, or six concerts to be presented in the coming season "to augment the great cultural needs of the community." Then a dinner for the workers climaxes the drive, at which time the grand total of monies collected is announced. Then the committee and the organizer select such talent as the available budget can accommodate. Of course, the staff member is mainly interested in selling his own company's artists; but by dint of persistence and insistence artists of other bureaus can be secured. The original idea was sound, but when the system encroached on the territory of established independent managers, then it was carrying things too far. Eventually we were surrounded by eight such organized concert series in towns not ten miles away, organized and promoted by the very agencies from whom we were booking most of our talent.

Even Henry Ford gave his dealers franchises and determined the locations of his other dealers so that they would not encroach on each other. Also he stuck to manufacturing and let others handle the business of selling the merchandise. *Time* magazine's feature story of this development in the music world called it "Chain-Store Music" and stated further that "to the few independent managers who can subsist on the crumbs that Columbia and NBC let fall, the wholesale chains are objects of mingled horror and envy." Today there are comparatively few independent concert managements remaining throughout the country. Also, it has been estimated that more than one-half of the thireen hundred organized concert units have now disbanded.

The most exciting new personality to come over from Europe about this time was Ljuba Welitch, a sensational Viennese dramatic soprano who became a member of the Metropolitan Opera Company. Very seldom does any concert artist stop a show, but twice she had to repeat a number before continuing. Her *Salome* at the Metropolitan Opera was sold out far in advance and as often as it was scheduled. We were fortunate in being able to sponsor one of her few concerts in America.

Two-piano teams were becoming more frequent after the success of the English duo pianists Ethel Bartlett and Rae Robertson. Their joint recitals opened up a rich treasure house of music, and their warm personalities endeared them to audiences. We repeated them several times and eventually introduced Luboshutz and Nemenoff, Vronsky and Babin, and other masters of four-hand piano playing.

Other than Kreisler, there were only two violinists who were repeated from time to time — Heifetz and Menuhin. A prodigy at the age of ten, Menuhin was seventeen when he first appeared in the Olney series. He had already been soloist with ten leading symphony orchestras. The technically flawless Heifetz was a fixture with elite music lovers. But his box-office appeal did not approach that of Kreisler, although he always required a similar fee.

An interesting article appeared on the front page of the *Wall Street Journal* in 1951 (our nineteenth season). It was headlined, "Serious Music: America, Land of Jazz Turns Out to Be Lover of the Symphony, Too. $45 Million-a-Year Receipts of 'Long Hair' Events Surpass Baseball Gate." Author Stanley Klegfield stated that 30 million people had paid money to attend performances of serious music that year. Symphony orchestras had increased in number all over the country. Sol Hurok stated that program reform had been in part responsible for the serious music spree; and we were quoted as being partial to the theory that the U.S. is reaching cultural maturity. However, the organized audience plan was credited with presenting eight thousand concerts in many towns of less than 500,000 population. The growth of ballet and opera, though less spectacular, was impressive.

The Sadlers Wells Ballet drew $19,266 for us on the final performance of its first tour of the United States, thereby breaking all receipts and attendance records. One of the truly fabulous touring attractions of our time, its performance of *The Sleeping Beauty* rates as one of the most memorable theater events of our recollection. With each new Hurok importation one always knew there would be a solid publicity buildup so that, long before it reached America, our public would know about the event. This anticipation was always an immense help in building public interest in a new attraction.

The return of Flagstad in January 1951 was a reminder of her concert in December 1935, after her first sensational season at the Metropolitan. We had signed her immediately after her debut and found that here was an extraordinary new concert artist to present. Her husband had come from Europe to White Plains for this concert. He was absolutely jubilant at her success and was heard to remark, "Look, with that enormous voice, you still cannot see her breathe at all."

The edge was somewhat taken off her concert fifteen years later, however, when we were called at two o'clock on the afternoon of her appearance and told she had severe laryngitis. It was too late to reach the afternoon papers, but radio announcements were made and telegrams sent out to all season subscribers. Less than fifty people turned up at the County Center auditorium that night, and everyone accepted the inevitable in good spirit. When Mme Flagstad finally filled the postponed engagement, she was again in good voice and every bit the superb singer in the grand manner—made of the same heroic mould as Melchior.

At the close of the 1951 season, we announced transfer of our presentations in the future to RKO Keith's Theatre. After twenty years of usage, the County Center auditorium was run down, maintenance was careless, and many complaints were received from subscribers. Not the least of these were the hard chairs on the main floor. The Recreation Commission refused to face conditions but, instead, raised the rent and curtailed services. Thus the County Center lost its most prestigious tenant.

The theater had only one-half as many seats, but they were new and comfortable. Other facilities were well maintained, and the atmosphere was more intimate. Also, with the trend away from recitals to ballet and ensemble attractions, this theater offered superior stage accommodations and box-office arrangements.

The Olney series, however, was destined to continue for only two more full seasons. In this period an effort was made to recapture the momentum lost during wartime with the introduction of more ensemble attractions. In the final season there were no solo recitalists. But the policy proved even more expensive, and other costs of operation were steadily mounting. The encroachment of the Community Concert Series in surrounding towns helped to deplete season subscriptions by nearly one-half. Also, the day had passed when there was a choice of big-name artists. No more was there available a galaxy of celebrated artists, built up by devoted personal managers, such as there had been in 1930.

So, on the morning of March 26, 1953, after the last concert of the Olneys' twentieth season, the *New York Times* wrote, "After a twenty-year run, a regularly scheduled concert season came to an end tonight when the Olney management presented the Robert Shaw Chorale of thirty singers, accompanied by an orchestra of twenty players, before an audience of 2500 at the RKO Keith Theatre."

The attraction was so overpriced that the concert lost $1,200 and confirmed our decision to abandon an operation that had provided many rewarding experiences but had apparently outlived its usefulness.

5

The World Crisis

"Wherever the path may lead, we shall travel it more prosperously and more safely if we English-speaking people travel it together."
—Rt. Hon. Winston Churchill

The outstanding lecture attraction for the season 1931–1932 was the first (also the last) American tour of the Rt. Hon. Winston Churchill.

When we inquired of his Boston management the amount of the eminent statesman's fee, we were informed it was $2,500. So, we dropped the matter. Mr. Churchill, at that time, was out of public life; in fact, it was generally considered that his achievements and career were already quite beyond those of most current heads of state. Statesman, author, and soldier, he had seen service in the Boer War; he served a quarter of a century in Parliament; in World War I he had been minister of munitions and then first lord of the admiralty; and, under Stanley Baldwin, he served as chancellor of the exchequer.

Very early in the tour Mr. Churchill had the unfortunate taxi accident on Fifth Avenue in New York City that necessitated hospitalization and threw his lecture schedule out of kilter. Most of the engagements were filled on postponed dates; but there was one open date remaining at the end of the revised schedule. It was offered to us for $1,000, with the result that we sponsored his last public appearance in this country, for which tickets could be bought by the general public.

Late in the afternoon of March 8, 1932, Mr. Churchill drove out from New York City, accompanied by a sergeant from Scotland Yard. They brought supper and picnicked en route along the Bronx River Parkway. Everything possible was done to make the occasion auspicious. Gen. James G. Harbord, chairman of the Radio Corporation of America, was secured to introduce the speaker. An outstanding general officer of World War I, he had been a friend and admirer of Mr. Churchill's.

In introducing the British statesman, General Harbord said, "I know of no living man who has had such a wide sweep of experience in so many different lines — any one of which would have furnished the average man an ample theater for an entire career. . . . In his very early twenties he saw military service on four continents. . . . To his wisdom as first lord of the admiralty the world owes the fact that the British Grand Fleet was in the right place in the first week of August, 1914. In Parliament for a quarter of the century, a member of the cabinets of half a dozen British governments, the prime of life finds him a central and commanding figure — in British public life unrivalled.

"I very well recall the last time I saw him. Gen. Pershing and I, who had ridden in the great Victory Parade of July 1919, were at Westminster that night for dinner. Mr. Churchill . . . was a member of the group at our table and, at the end of the dinner, charmed us with a prophetic vision, with a yellow tinge, of which events now happening in the Orient are a reminder."

Mr. Churchill's analysis of the pending world crisis and his prognostication of things to come were almost uncanny. Among other things, he stated that, "Peace and disarmament are cherished by both the United States and Britain, but it would be a pity if the English-speaking people were the only one to disarm and something happens to the peace. . . . If the world is to accept the present misery, it must have some created nucleus. There is a world force ready to take the primacy of nations. That is Communism."

"On our side," he continued, "are 150 millions of men and women spread over the globe, representing places abounding in wealth and power, progress and the capacity for progress, the most harmonious grouping of the human race since the Roman Empire. There are seven thousand miles of new frontiers. In the

Roman world 800,000 soldiers kept the peace. Today, in Europe, 20 millions of soldiers guard the jigsaw of twenty-six different frontiers. . . . We should band to have the 'instrumentality' (President Wilson's word) adequate to defend our rights and discharge our duties. By having this instrumentality we could prevent or localize almost any quarrel among men. . . . You might say the force of right backed by the right of force."

Mr. Churchill then submitted to questions from the audience. Some of the answers were well worth the price of admission by themselves. This account of one of these was taken from the *New York Times* of March 9. To a question as to whether Russia had contributed anything to world progress, Mr. Churchill replied, "Not half as much as to world disaster."

The affair drew a half-page editorial in the White Plains *Reporter* signed by W. Livingston Larned. Many years later it is interesting now to recall a portion of his writing.

> Winston Churchill has led a distinguished and useful career . . . the son of a woman of our own soil and an English nobleman. . . . It is significant in view of the strange misunderstanding which has seemed to exist, and persist, for far too long between his country and ours. Perhaps it will take a vast, common cause, such as a world upheaval, to bring us together. The crisis seems to be on the horizon. It is the ancient conflict between education and ignorance; paganism and Christianity; the white races against yellow, brown, and black. Frontiers glow with the fires of hatred and suspicion. If there is to be a survival of civilization, it will mean a closer bond between those who have fostered it, made it possible, those who brought it into existence.
>
> Winston Churchill came to us on a mission of good fellowship. Genial, witty, sympathetic, he would rip down the ugly barriers that separate us and encourage the ideal that, of all peoples, we two belong shoulder to shoulder.

In the midst of the agonies of World War II, almost nine years later, Winston Churchill's prophetic speech on the world crisis was to be recalled in the New York metropolitan press. A picture taken when he spoke for us was reproduced in the *New York Times*. Oddly enough, the event had drawn the season's slimmest audience, and the sponsors lost several hundred dollars. But the occasion had quality plus, even if the auditors on hand were lacking in number.

All the words quoted in this chapter were said or written in 1932. Now, to the added stature gained by Sir Winston Churchill for his achievements as prime minister during World War II, are added his voluminous writings, which will forever be a permanent contribution to the English literature and historic writing of all time.

6

Other Special Events

*"I have pitched so many
dreams out of the window
that one more or less
makes little difference."*
—Bernard Shaw

Certain special events and presentations are worth mentioning in passing. The concert subscription series was a steady
grosser from year to year, but the margin was never enough.

Home base for the Olney presentations since the beginning
had been the main auditorium of the Westchester County
Center in White Plains. The prime reason that had led to the
erection of this building in the first place was the need for
permanent facilities to house the annual Westchester Music
Festival. For many years it was held every May under a tent
pitched at the base of the Kensico Reservoir Dam just north of
White Plains. Mrs. Eugene Meyer, Jr., of Mt. Kisco had been
the guiding spirit in bringing together choruses from all over
Westchester County to sing in this annual event. Important
solo artists also participated, and much enthusiasm was
engendered by all concerned.

It was Mrs. Meyer who then sold the idea of building the
Westchester County Center to William L. Ward, political
leader of the county. The festival continued for some years
under the direction of the Recreation Commission, which
successfully directed its destinies throughout its first years in the
new County Center. Through gradual replacements, however,

the caliber of the Commission personnel declined, and so did the fortunes of the annual music festival.

Through the leadership of a few public-spirited citizens, Mrs. Valentine E. Macy was persuaded to accept the chairmanship of a committee to rehabilitate and continue the excellent work of this festival. She set to work and immediately secured Hugh Ross as musical director and the Olneys as managers. And, so the twelfth annual Westchester Music Festival was reestablished and announced for May 8 and 9, 1936. It was produced on a rather modest scale, using mainly the massed group of county choruses, with soloists and members of the New York Philharmonic Orchestra for accompaniment.

The next season the number of programs was expanded to three evening concerts. The principal innovation was use of the Philadelphia Orchestra, with Eugene Ormandy conducting one of the concerts. Receipts were up about 50 percent over the preceding year, but expenses were up even more. Artistically the festival was built back into a first-class event, but the general public was not intrigued in sufficient numbers. Haydn's *Creation* was given a splendid rendition one year, followed by Bach's B Minor Mass the next season.

The festival was continued for a third season in 1938 by "Happy" Macy and her committee. She worked untiringly and was an inspiration to the choruses and all concerned, but it would have been unfair to expect her to continue also raising the deficit money year after year. This item seemed to have become stabilized in the vicinity of five thousand dollars. A farsighted recreation commission should have continued to handle this event and appropriate the relatively modest sum needed out of its annual budget. And so one of the country's notable annual festivals was allowed to lapse.

Some extra events took the form of benefits. One of the most exciting was the program we assembled and managed for British War Relief at the County Center in October 1941. For the first and only time there was presented in joint concert the United States Marine Band with Gracie Fields as solo performer. This was a rare combination, indeed, and most appropriate for the purpose.

One of the sensational entertainers of all time, Gracie Fields had recently come to America. Originally from the Lancashire district, Gracie was the idol of the working classes, and in time her earnings as an entertainer topped those of any other English performer. Her knack with a song was uncanny. Who could ever forget "Walter, Walter (Lead Me to the Altar)," "He's Dead—But He Won't Lie Down," "An Old Violin," "Nighty-Night, Little Sailor Boy," "The Biggest Aspidistra in the World," and others? Gracie was full of odd impulses and, on occasion, would startle the audience by suddenly doing a cartwheel in the middle of a song, then would continue with the number just as though nothing unusual had taken place.

Among those on hand was a large delegation of sailors from the British Maritime Service occupying a block of seats donated by a patron. One of the group happened to be a survivor from the submarine sinking of a British merchant vessel—the S. S. Gracie Fields—in the retreat from Dunkirk. During intermission he went backstage and presented Gracie with his hat band, which bore the name of the ship. As a further coincidence, it turned out that both the singer and the sailor hailed from the same hometown back in England. She was greatly overcome, and it made a touching story when she told the audience about it immediately after intermission.

Altogether the event was a gala occasion and garnered a handsome five-figure gross in receipts for a noble cause.

Lily Pons headlined a concert benefit for the Judson Health Center, which we put on at the Metropolitan Opera House in April 1935. Such an event required extensive advance work, and the expenses were considerable. At the high prices charged, much of the ticket selling had to be done through well-organized committees. The petite prima donna from France was in her prime, and the event was an artistic as well as a financial success.

Another promotion, very much on the commercial side, was the Memorial Day service put on for the benefit of the Ferncliff Mausoleum in May 1940. It was a huge success, and this record would not be complete without it. The directors of this place had recently erected a costly marble mausoleum and still had building plans that required fulfillment.

So we devised a program that drew a crowd of over ten

thousand and got good coverage in the metropolitan press. Eleanor Roosevelt was secured for the principal speaker, and a program of organ and choral music was arranged by Caroline Beeson Fry, with James Melton as soloist.

Elaborately engraved invitations went out to all leading federal government officials in the New York metropolitan area as well as to foreign consular officials. Out of deference to the president's wife, most of them accepted, with the result that those on hand included Gen. Hugh A. Drum, Rr. Adm. Clark Howell Woodward, Maj. Gen. John F. O'Ryan, and many others. Hon. William F. Bleakley introduced the speaker. Hon. Charles D. Millard was chairman, and Mrs. William D. Sporborg was vice-chairman.

Consuls were present from Argentina, Bulgaria, China, Cuba, Denmark, Czechoslovakia, Ecuador, Finland, France, Great Britain, Greece, Liberia, Nicaragua, Paraguay, Poland, Portugal, Rumania, Spain, Switzerland, Venezuela, and Yugoslavia.

As headliner for the program, Mrs. Roosevelt was paid a fee of $1,500 out of the total budget of $10,000. The subject of her talk was, "The Significant Challenge of Memorial Day This Year."

Another form of presentation undertaken was to handle professional tennis matches. That game probably requires more practice and outright skill than any other form of athletic activity. Also, it is certainly one of the most thrilling of spectator sports, which is why we failed to understand its current status as a minor sport.

Tennis, as a form of sports competition, only recently has been gaining stature comparable to golf and some other sports. The current phase of major exhibition tours was started in the season of 1951-1952 under the aegis of Jack Harris. The featured players were Jack Kramer and Bobby Riggs, supported by Pancho Segura and Dinny Pails. Harris did a great job in booking the tours throughout America as well as in other countries. But when they reached Australia, the boys figured that he was collecting too much of the receipts and decided to take over and manage themselves.

Only in comparatively recent years has tennis become better

organized, with attractive purses for the players. And the sport can now boast a World Championship Tennis competition. These were goals that I had advocated back in the late 1930s.

I continued with the matches for three seasons, playing them in Springfield and Hartford, Connecticut; Newark, Albany, Syracuse, and other cities in New York, in addition to the regular matches at the County Center in White Plains. In fact, I handled most of the eastern playing time outside of the big arenas in Boston, New York, and Philadelphia.

Jack Kramer, heading up pro tennis in the 1940s, was not unappreciative and wrote me that "you have always done such a good job. . . . Our sincerest thanks for the wonderful way you handled our matches for us," etc. Also "I want to take this opportunity to tell you how much we appreciated the wonderful job you did. . . . When it comes to promoting there just isn't anyone who can do a better job. . . . It's a real pleasure to do business with you each year."

It was during this same period that we had extended our activities to other cities in the New England area and as far south as Washington, D.C., and so became regional managers. We would take important touring attractions on a multicity basis on the most favorable terms possible. This tendency has become more and more evident in different sections of the country as professional managements find it increasingly difficult to come out on presentations when confined to one city. In fact, new towns have been discovered in this way that have turned out to be more lucrative than some of the big cities, where the public has become saturated and the local expenses have risen to astronomical heights.

Although we had always shied away from the management of talent itself, we did arrange several tours for individual artists. The first was in the fall of 1934, when I booked my first tour, which also happened to be the last joint tour of the famed adventurers Mr. and Mrs. Martin Johnson. We had done a good job in presenting them two years previously, so they wrote from Nairobi in Kenya Colony, asking us to arrange their future appearances. The title of the new Johnsons' lecture–film was "Wings Over Africa," and their performance fee was $1,000—a top sum at that time.

They were the first explorers to systematically employ airplanes to photographing the natural wonders and wildlife of the African continent. His penchant for flying was to cost Martin his life after returning to America from their next African safari. His plane was wrecked over the Tehachapi Mountains just north of Los Angeles. Osa escaped with severe injuries but managed bravely to fulfill the lecture-tour commitments from a wheelchair.

Some years later, after the first reading tour had been booked for Charles Laughton, I carried on with the booking of his programs. Eventually they brought in fees totaling over $300,000. I also made two national tours for Agnes Moorehead, whose delightful program was climaxed with the thriller *Sorry, Wrong Number*. The program material was selected and directed by Charles Laughton and was most successful.

Among attractions we first introduced to eastern audiences in the early 1950s were Bernard Shaw's *Don Juan in Hell* and Stephen Vincent Benét's *John Brown's Body*, both of which were played throughout the New England area. This was to be the beginning of our association with Charles Laughton and Paul Gregory. And it was at this point that we were to become national managers as well as presenters of stage attractions in many new cities. Now our base of operations was removed to Hollywood.

The last individual tour undertaken was for the lovely ballerina Tamara Toumanova in 1956. She had first appeared under our auspices twenty-one years previous as a featured ballerina with the Ballet Russe de Monte Carlo. As the result of a highly successful ballet recital given in the Los Angeles Philharmonic Auditorium, we took on the touring of a ballet recital for Toumanova with an assisting artist accompanied by two pianos. She garnered first-class notices and proved herself one of the outstanding artists of our time and a person of real charm and intelligence.

Probably the most difficult, as well as the most intriguing, national campaign ever undertaken by our office was Dorothy's effort on a big scale to sell *Pictura—Adventure in Art*. This magnificent film was planned and produced by Leonid Kipnis and Hermann Starr.

In six parts, it was based on the lives and works of Hieronymus Bosch, Vittore Carpaccio, Paul Gauguin, Francisco Goya, Henri de Toulouse-Lautrec, and Grant Wood. The six parts were narrated by Vincent Price, Henry Fonda, Martin Gabel, Harry Marble, Lilli Palmer, and Gregory Peck—all with special musical accompaniment. The Toulouse-Lautrec and Gauguin sequences were made in France; Bosch, Carpaccio, and Goya in Italy; and Grant Wood in the United States.

The high caliber and entertainment value of this remarkable feature art film was expressed by Francis Henry Taylor, late director of the Metropolitan Museum of Art in New York when he wrote, "I found myself completely entranced with the wonders of this picture—a production which provides fascinating entertainment and real excitement for the movie-goer."

Pictura was first played for a selected number of key runs in important art theaters in Los Angeles, New York, Chicago, San Francisco, and Washington. Then, provided with rave reviews, it was decided to sell it entirely by mail to museums, clubs, and cultural organizations from coast to coast. This was done by means of an attractive mailing packet that was expensive to produce but brought results.

The mailing piece proved irresistible and resulted in bookings coming from across the country for a very special high-class art picture that had only a limited appeal at the outset.

7

The Lost Festival

"If only the basic plans, as outlined by
the Fair's Music Committee, are realized
the program will be the most significant
ever presented in this country."
—Mrs. Vincent Astor (Mrs. Lytle Hull)

It was early in 1937 that plans for the 1939 New York World's Fair began to be activated in earnest. Having successfully launched a major concert subscription series jointly with Dorothy, assisted in management of the Ridgeway Theatre, and then produced a rejuvenated Westchester Music Festival, I was ready for a new challenge.

Through Jay Downer, formerly chief engineer for the Westchester Park Commission and then engineer for Rockefeller Center and consultant to the World's Fair, I met Grover Whalen. Soon, thereafter, I was appointed by Allen Wardwell to be Executive Secretary of the Music Advisory Committee for the Fair. An unusually happy choice for the chairmanship of this impressive group, Mr. Wardwell was most understanding and exceptionally qualified for the post. Unfortunately, he had to take a leave of absence for health reasons, so it devolved on Mrs. Vincent Astor to carry on.

Possessed of considerable personal charm and a measure of independence, Mrs. Astor took an intense interest in the work ahead. After all, music had always been a deep-seated life interest, and she was not long in becoming aware of the extraordinary potential in this new opportunity.

43

An early statement made by Mrs. Astor is worth quoting from "The Olney Prompter" of March 11, 1938.

> For the first time in the history of American expositions, music, as projected for the New York World's Fair in 1939, is to occupy a really important place. All this, of course, is in line with the vast increase in music interest throughout this country in recent years, largely stimulated by the radio. America, and particularly the New York area, has, in fact, become the music capital of the world—just as certainly as it is the financial capital. And, with the increasing unrest abroad, and the concentration in this country of more and more musical talent, there is no question as to the kind of music representation which should take place at the New York World's Fair. . . .
>
> In order to realize its greatest potentialities, of course, the program must be essentially international in character. To this end, each country will have an opportunity to bring to the attention of not only America, but also the world, that which is to be regarded as the very essence of its particular musical genius. But the emphasis should be upon all the aspects, past and present, of America's very rich musical life, and all parts of the United States should be represented, not only by orchestras and glee clubs and the like, but also by the folk music and dances and the popular music of the different parts of the country, and, indeed, of all the Western Hemisphere.

Among the several plans that had been early submitted to the fair management for consideration was an elaborate music program outlined by Olin Downes, music critic of the *New York Times*. It was an utterly impractical proposal, and he was more than a little piqued when another program was adopted later on. In any event, it was in their first meeting that Mr. Wardwell and I had taken cognizance of the Downes situation and agreed that every effort should be made to retain his interest and to influence his efforts into more helpful channels.

Instructions to the Advisory Committee on Music from the World's Fair directors included the following:

> The functions of this Committee will be to advise the New York World's Fair Corporation on all matters relating to a program of classical music at the Fair. . . . This Committee will be asked to prepare and recommend to the Fair Corporation a

plan of musical programs to be presented within the Fair grounds in keeping with the facilities for such a program as will be provided. . . . It is hoped that a . . . musical program along the foregoing lines will be prepared and presented that will be without precedent in the history of this City.

The composition of the committee was made up of those who stood out foremost in the rich musical life of the great city. Although the large and impressive committee was most prestigious, the real work of devising a suitable program was carried on by the chairman with the help of subcommittee chairmen and, especially, the executive committee. Fully attended meetings could only take place at long intervals. As it was important at the outset to get ideas and ascertain sentiment, I personally consulted with nearly every member of the committee. The contacts were stimulating and useful and produced a vast range of suggestions and opinions. These were summarized in reports and formed the basis of the program which was put in final form under the direction of Dr. Walter Damrosch. It was approved by the music advisory committee on November 9, 1937, and then adopted by the fair's directorate the following January.

The language used by the distinguished Dr. Damrosch in presenting the report of his program committee is well worth recording here.

I found the Committee from the very beginning remarkably harmonious and unanimous. It was composed principally of musicians and critics and I must say that the lions, which were the critics, and the lambs, which were the musicians, have sat down and lay down together in perfect amity and in general the conclusions adopted were that emphasis should be laid on the musical activities of Greater New York; that the cornerstone should be our two great institutions, the Metropolitan Opera Company and the Philharmonic Symphony Orchestra.

The New York World's Fair of 1939 provides an unprecedented opportunity whereby a great international festival of music may be realized in this country.

The summer of 1939 will find New York a magnet for all the nations. It will be the scene of the greatest international gathering in all history. And, of all the languages to be

45

represented, but one will be comprehensive to all alike—that of music. Here, for once, is a real opportunity to demonstrate the unifying influence of this foremost of the arts.

In a way the meeting today is historic. We have gathered here representatives of those several important musical institutions for which New York is already famous. For the first time, I feel we have come together to unite our efforts in a single purpose. We are going to prove not only that here, on this island, is located the financial capital of world industry, but also that New York is cultured and that here is centered the musical life of the world as well.

It is not at all unlikely that Olin Downes took umbrage at this report, for he had written in disparaging terms about Damrosch's music only the year before. A brilliant writer who commanded a sparkling verbiage in expressing his thoughts on music and musicians, Downes nevertheless had his prejudices. In my original report, detailing my interview with him, the following notations are of interest:

According to Mr. Downes, there are only fifteen good people on the Committee and there should be enough other names added so as to balance with the useless names. He has absolutely no use for managers, especially Arthur Judson whose ethics he questioned. Among his other prejudices are especially Mrs. Astor and Dr. Damrosch. He does not think he was too hard on Dr. Damrosch last spring but he hopes the editorial he had run a few days later may have helped to ameliorate that situation.

In spite of this attitude, Downes eventually managed to so influence Mrs. Astor (neither the music advisory committee nor its executive committee was ever consulted) that he was appointed director of music when the Fair Corporation implemented the music program a month after its adoption. At the same time I was then appointed music manager. The proposed new program was hailed in the press and other periodicals from coast to coast.

Mr. Downes was presumably the artistic head of the enterprise while it would be my job to translate everything into action—to manage and to promote the festival. We had desks at opposite ends of a beautifully furnished capacious new office.

46

For Downes it was luxury, compared with the almost monastic cubicle he occupied at the *New York Times*. He loved to press buttons that placed messengers and secretaries at his beck and call. Once he remarked that he should be drawing the kind of money Arthur Judson earned, and vice versa.

Now Downes was in the position of arranging and selecting talent for a unique music festival while at the same time he functioned as critic of the *New York Times*. In the meantime, I had been on the job for a year, and the foundation had been laid for a great international festival. A program had been formulated and approved, an appropriation of $350,000 voted for construction of a music hall, and a department of music created within the fair's own organization.

During the year preceding there had been many discussions over the physical facilities that would be available. Originally, it was assumed that Robert Moses' Marine Amphitheater would be home base for the fair's concerts and music events; but this proved to be impractical. Had Moses listened to John Golden and other authorities who knew much more about the implications, he would have gone for the plan of a large, enclosed auditorium on the order of the Westchester County Center. The Marine Amphitheater cost more than twice as much and proved to be less than half as useful because it could not be utilized throughout the winter season.

Installed in his new post, Downes became overbearing and impractical. I finally decided to take a leave of absence, then resigned, although I retained my post on the Music Advisory Committee at Mrs. Astor's request. As a part-time music consultant, which was the capacity in which Downes had been expected to serve, his efforts would not have been incompatible with his main job of a newspaper critic.

As was to be expected, Downes was helpless as a babe when it came to implementing the program adopted by the music advisory committee and which was subsequently confirmed by the fair's directors. He was completely lacking in management and promotion know-how, negotiating contracts, etc. Eventually the program fell into disarray. After all, one does not become a presenter overnight any more than a pianist learns his craft in a month, or a year, or in several years. It would have been just as presumptuous for me to have attempted writing music criticism.

In this connection, Downes wrote to Mrs. Astor in Palm Beach,

> I am deeply gratified that Mr. Olney has consented to continue this arrangement because I feel it would be greatly to the disadvantage of the whole musical arrangements of the Fair if a man of his experience, capacities, and character were to be lost to us in this connection. For my own part, if this arrangement can be assured, I shall have great happiness in the continued cooperation of Mr. Olney, who is such a sincere and uncompromising worker for the ideal, a man of achievement and a true gentleman.

From Palm Beach, Mrs. Astor wrote me,

> I am always appreciative of what you did in starting off the Music Advisory Committee and hope you will continue as its secretary.

Tributes to my efforts were paid also by Dr. Damrosch and Marshall Field.

Downes's part-time efforts on behalf of the music program were, of course, abortive (he was still critic of the *New York Times*, a full-time job). For nearly a year the Music Advisory Committee was not called into session. When it did meet again on January 25, 1939, it was mainly for the purpose of hearing a program report by Music Director Downes, who had been in office nearly a full year.

Through nearly one-half hour of glowing rhetoric, he outlined project after project—a few completely set up, a few in negotiation, but most merely vague promises. In short, the program was so broad it would have had to be expanded into other facilities throughout the city of New York. None of the many projects outlined at this session were ever realized.

Two weeks later, a telegram went out from Mrs. Astor to every member of the committee, summoning them to an emergency meeting at her home. On the day following that meeting I sent in my resignation to the chairman "inasmuch as there was no plan evolved or steps taken at the emergency meeting" to realize the program adopted and then approved by the fair directorate over a year before.

On February 23, 1939, Allen Wardwell wrote me, saying, among other things, "I am sorry the whole program has dwindled down to such an extent . . . and, of course, . . . I am sorry that your connection with the music program did not work out for I thought we always worked very well together and I had great hopes that some portion of the program we originally discussed could have been accomplished."

The Downes's debacle was in great contrast to the masterful presentation by Dr. Damrosch of the original ambitious program in November 1937. In passing, it should be noted for the record that this grand figure in American music conducted the preview concert on the World's Fair grounds, featuring Beethoven's Ninth Symphony. This took place just forty-five years after he had led the New York Philharmonic at the World's Fair in Chicago near the close of the last century.

It was one of the phenomena of World's Fair publicity that the collapse of its music program received scarcely a passing notice in the New York press. All in all, however, this was a gigantic operation, and probably it should be put down to the credit of the newspapers that this and other shortcomings were bypassed in the interests of the main project of putting over the fair itself.

The Inaugural Concert at the fair was given on April 30, 1939, with John Barbirolli conducting the New York Philharmonic Symphony and featuring Josef Hofmann as piano soloist. A few national concerts followed that programmed music of Great Britain, Norway, Brazil, Finland, Rumania, and other countries. But it was not long before the fair's Music Hall was turned over to Mike Todd and his girl shows—entertainment in a somewhat more popular vein.

All through the several committee sessions, Minnie Guggenheimer, chairman of the annual stadium concerts, had sat quietly poised and had little to say except to put in a plug here and there for her regular season to take place at the Lewisohn Stadium. As it turned out, she was to engage me for her manager during the ten-week summer season of 1939.

At the opening stadium concert on June 14, Mayor LaGuardia conducted the "Star-Spangled Banner," after which Dr. Damrosch conducted the regular concert, with Albert Spalding as violin soloist. Then followed symphonic concerts featuring notable soloists; ballet, choral, and opera performances; and a full Beethoven Cycle. There were also national concerts performing the music of Russia, Finland, Germany, France, Switzerland, and Czechoslovakia.

And so there was an International Festival of Music after all, but it was brought into being at the Lewisohn Stadium across the East River from the World's Fair itself.

8

Concerts under the Stars

> *"Taken individually, the people in an audience may be all poor critics of music, but as a complete body the audience never errs. It is never wrong in its reaction to a performance."*
> —*Rachmaninoff*

This title may infer soothing symphonies, sweet romance, and a general state of bliss and forgetfulness—all on a summer's evening—but what dismal affairs concerts can be when the skies are teeming! Many times, in opening the door of the two-by-four manager's office offstage at the Lewisohn Stadium in New York City, it was to admit members of the distaff side soaked to the skin from a sudden downpour. There was literally no shelter available once the skies had decided to unleash their burden and drench the huge amphitheater.

Outdoor concerts present plenty of hazards under any conditions—financial loss, talent cancellations, transportation problems, etc. But they all pale into comparative insignificance when the weather goes on a rampage. The management, of course, always and invariably maintained a pose of optimism until the water actually was descending in quantity and defeat was inevitable. Once the decision to cancel was made, I pulled the emergency switch beside my desk, which flashed a red light on either side of the orchestra's canopy. Within almost less time than it requires to tell about it, the audience of thousands had scattered to no one quite knew where—the stands were desolated so fast and so thoroughly.

Occasionally, if the rainmaker let up shortly or appeared hesitant about administering a further ducking, the management would quickly regain optimism and flash on the green lights. Then, swiftly and silently, another miracle occurred: the audience suddenly reappeared, assembled from all the stores, building entrances, autos, and other odd corners of the neighborhood whence they had fled. Papers and wraps were spread over the wet seats, and the business of the evening proceeded very much as usual.

Even with the help of Dr. Kimball and his competent weather department downtown, one could never be quite sure just what to expect. In the summer of 1940 there was the evening with about twelve thousand persons on hand in the audience when the first ballet program of the season was to be presented. The skies were black and threatening, but still it hadn't actually rained. At the starting time of 8:30 P.M. questions regarding whether we were going ahead with the program were already being asked. The orchestra was tuning up an overture (the string section under some protest) when Conductor Smallens was sent on from his offside entrance. Just as Alex raised his arms to signal the opening bars, the skies loosed a torrent. The rainmaker meant business this time, so there was not the slightest room left for doubt: the program had to be canceled fast.

On still another occasion, with the conditions almost identical, Heifetz was slated for soloist. Inasmuch as the artist was already on hand and maintaining a remarkably imperturbable front, there was not too much concern and it was decided to proceed as usual. The crowd was large and expectant, and Jascha had interrupted a vacation to which he was anxious to return. Opening time of 8:30 P.M. arrived, and the skies again were dark and threatening. As the conductor raised his baton, a few scattered large drops of rain came down, the usual prelude to another deluge.

A few people were already starting toward the exits. Nevertheless, while the weather continued to threaten all through the evening, the deluge never arrived (at least not until midnight); the audience did remain, and another successful evening was added to the annals of stadium concerts.

From a purely musical standpoint, the notices in the metropolitan press on the day following were extraordinary. Heifetz had played everything as scheduled, his costly instrument exposed to the weather, and had delivered one of the artistic triumphs of his entire career. And, it must be added, he had not appeared to be at all disturbed during the entire program.

This was somewhat in contrast to our experience with Mischa Elman in the preceding season. During the afternoon of the cloudy, humid, threatening day of his scheduled appearance, he was insistent on canceling. But, until 8:30 P.M., several hours still remained in which the weatherman might readily change his tactics. The performance did come off, in any event, but Elman still thought it should have been canceled.

Chairwoman Guggenheimer thoroughly embarrassed me on one occasion. On a date scheduled for the first ballet engagement of one summer season it appeared as though the rainmaker was desperately trying to extinguish the fires of hell all morning—New York was drenched. By noontime she decided to cancel out and postpone the performance. Press and radio were so notified. Nevertheless, by midafternoon there was not a cloud to be seen, the sky was the clearest and deepest of blues. It was a hasty and impulsive decision, but she was always difficult to advise, and efforts to reinstate the program made no impression. Then, of course, it was risky to be too emphatic about it—after all, it could be raining again by evening.

The performance, however, had been well-publicized. Ballet was becoming more and more a popular attraction, and I had visions of turning away thousands of irate customers under a cloudless sky with the unconvincing excuse that it had rained in the morning. And that was exactly the situation that had to be faced. Thousands of patrons (estimated at between five and six thousand) turned up to storm the great iron gates. Even though the box office would have suffered from a diminished attendance, the show should have gone on.

The original idea for the Lewisohn Stadium concerts was conceived by Mrs. Arnold Volpe and her late conductor husband in 1918. She once wrote to me,

> Little did we dream when we brought the idea to Mr. and Mrs. Charles Guggenheimer that we were making musical history for the advancement, appreciation and growth of music in America. . . . The concerts proved successful from the first and were given for seven weeks, fifty concerts in all. . . . Receipts for the first year were $31,959.26 and disbursements $41,247.27. The programs included symphony nights, opera in concert form with the Metropolitan Opera Chorus, nationality nights, etc. Mr. Volpe had to conduct seven performances a week with only two rehearsals, including one or more soloists for each night. Due to world conditions no works by German composers including Wagner could be performed. . . . During the second year receipts and attendance were doubled.

Since that time receipts from ticket sales more than quadrupled. To this revenue is added income from the concessions.

I was greatly interested when the opportunity came to take on the management of the famous stadium concerts after the bitter disappointment at the New York World's Fair in this same summer of 1939. After all, the stadium had been a going concern for twenty years and, in honor of the fair, it had been extended now from an eight-week to a ten-week gala season.

Actually, I was to be the working manager, although Arthur Judson was the general manager. His summers, however, were spent at his sumptuous camp on Lake Timagami in northern Ontario, and it was only rarely that he ever attended one of the concerts. Being manager of the New York Philharmonic Symphony Society, Judson's main interest was getting his orchestra signed up for the summer. "A.J." was also the president of Columbia Concerts Corporation.

A. J. did offer good, sound advice from time to time, which was, as often as not, disregarded by Mrs. Charles S. ("Minnie") Guggenheimer, chairwoman and moving spirit of the stadium concerts almost from the beginning. The effervescent Minnie raised the financing each spring with which to compensate for the anticipated summer deficit. She seldom, if ever, had formal meetings of the stadium concerts corporation board. Minutes,

54

contracts, and other legal papers were all handled down in her husband's law office. But she always had a plethora of advisers — social, professional, official, artistic, competent and incompetent.

Although the concerts were customarily presented during a limited eight-weeks season beginning in late June, their preparation and promotion was always a year-round task. Most important, solo talent had to be contracted about a year ahead; a contract had to be negotiated with the musicians' union; money gifts had to be promoted to defray the deficit; half a dozen conductors, more or less, had to be secured; advance ticket sales promoted, etc. Then committees, social and otherwise, to undertake various functions were formed and reformed.

The basis of the season had always been an orchestra of ninety-odd players, selected by Maurice Van Praag from the New York Philharmonic Symphony Society's personnel and paid one hundred dollars per week per man (except for the first desk positions). Usually on Monday and Thursday nights of each week solo artists were engaged for special performances, or perhaps ballet or opera performances would be presented. Rehearsals were held mornings; the more often conductors were changed, the more rehearsals were held. And at five hundred dollars per session (not counting overtime) this expense could mount up rapidly. Then, of course, there was the operating staff of seventy-odd persons — ticket sellers, ushers, gatemen, and cleaners.

That Minnie had been a sort of fairy godmother to these concerts, pouring in countless thousands of dollars over the years, was somewhat of a myth. In actual fact, a professional manager might have conducted the operation somewhat more economically. Under favorable conditions these concerts might have been made to "break" in a good season where an average of not more than one concert in a week was rained out. Nevertheless, they would inevitably go well into the red in any abnormally wet summer. Minnie's unflagging enthusiasm, however, was of inestimable value to the steady continuance of the concerts.

The average total season's receipts from ticket sales during the summers of 1939, 1940, and 1941, was $161,924. The balance of the $200,000 budget, more or less, was made up from contributions received from mail solicitation and through committee efforts.

The standard symphonic literature could be played through in a season, which made it desirable to play other works as well. But the royalties and extra instrumentation required for certain works by Respighi, Richard Strauss, and a few others having almost no draw have been known to absorb a large part of the box-office receipts, which would leave the basic expenses still to be met. On a program with Paul Robeson one evening, nearly one thousand dollars extra expense was incurred in order to try out a new ballad by a friend. It required training a special chorus and meant nothing but injection of fifteen minutes of boredom into an otherwise exciting program.

A business manager usually strives to make the best showing possible. But it was unlucky for the budget if Minnie was determined to secure a certain performer. Roses would be sent ahead, extra travel and other expenses paid, etc., then the fee would be probably tops. It must be added, however, that in some of her dealings Minnie was singularly astute. Years after the Gershwin Memorial Concert had become an established institution, Oscar Levant was still receiving hardly a token payment for his performance thereon. He was vital to the program, yet, on an evening in July 1940, when 16,741 persons paid $11,653.50 to hear him play the increasingly popular "Rhapsody in Blue," his check was for a mere $300.

There is always a dearth of smart new talent suitable for concert presentation. And, in addition to his talent, Oscar had personality as well as a "line." So, shortly after this appearance, I suggested to the leading concert managements that he should be toured for orchestra appearances. The result was his first tour the following season, on which the "Mrs. Julian Olney Series" in Westchester was included. He was presented as soloist with Artur Rodzinski and the Cleveland Orchestra. His fee added $1,250 to the cost of an already expensive concert.

The lengths to which someone will go, occasionally, to beat the management out of a fifty-cent or one-dollar admission are astonishing. So over the years a triple check system had been devised whereby, after handing in his ticket, each customer would pass through a turnstile which registered the total admissions. In addition to the regular box-office statement, therefore (made up by a bonded union treasurer), there was the turnstile count and then the ticket stubs, which were sorted and counted every evening. The normal season was seven nights a week for eight weeks, so the staff was seeing ticket stubs and turnstile readings in their sleep and did not feel too badly when a rainy night intervened and offered an occasional respite.

During the three seasons I was acting as manager for the stadium concerts, the total attendance was not far from running into seven figures. It is not possible to deal with so many people and not have many unique experiences, not to mention learning much about fellow human beings. The manager receives few bouquets and many threats, he meets numerous fine citizens and some fakirs, and most likely at the end he doesn't even rate a thank you.

There is nothing sadder or more forlorn than a theater or other place of entertainment just after a show has moved out or a season has been concluded. Everything is in disarray—papers and litter scattered about, seats overturned, and workmen dismantling the stage. And broken bottles are everywhere.

For some unfathomable reason, it was a source of pleasure to a certain segment of the patrons to break their soft drink bottles on the stone steps each night before departing. As a matter of fact, the cleaning crew had their own way of estimating the previous night's attendance. It bore a direct ratio, they said, to the quantity of broken glass retrieved, and usually they were not far wrong.

To the best of anyone's knowledge, I still hold the record for guessing stadium attendance. No matter whether the night was slow or the attendance heavy, members of the staff chipped in daily to a pool which went to the closest guess on the evening's attendance. One night I turned in an estimated figure of 8,000; the final count from the turnstiles came in at 8,001.

Minnie was, for many years, all things to the stadium. She delighted in telling others, even in front of the staff, how she was financier (she really was that), promoter (she was that only partially), press agent (only slightly), and manager (to some extent). Audiences learned to enjoy her quaint little talks from time to time; sometimes she even got a good laugh. But with all her faults it would be unkind not to give Minnie Guggenheimer due credit for carrying on year after year the task of seeing each season through to a conclusion. She always approached a new season with gusto—a spirit of real ardor, for she loved the work. She was unflagging in her efforts to set up the best season that could be arranged, and right after the last chord of "Auld Lang Syne" had melted into the summer air on the final night, she was already discussing her opening event for the following season.

Also, Minnie, for all her past performances, was still possessed of an adventuresome, even youthful, spirit. She was not above trying an occasional novelty, especially if it would bring any extra business to the box office. One of these occasions was the Gala Swiss Night during the New York World's Fair. For some curious reason it failed to draw business—in fact, the receipts were pitiful. But the occasion was unusually entertaining.

The first half of this program was entirely symphonic, the orchestra being led by Rudolph Ganz. At the close of the intermission, the entire stadium was completely darkened. As huge floodlights placed on the top of the stands at the rear were turned on, the varied assortment of costumed entertainers imported from Switzerland, who were to present the balance of the program, paraded around the field, then up onto the stadium stage. In the meantime, they were accompanied by a fife-and-drum corps that performed with remarkable spirit. Then followed exhibitions of folk dancing and singing; a potpourri of native melodies by a Swiss orchestra; Alp horn playing and flag throwing; the inevitable yodelers; and finally the fife-and-drum corps again. The latter was unquestionably the noisiest, yet most fascinating, aggregation ever seen in America. Wearing native costumes and standing erect and impassive, these drummers beat out their staccato measures in a thunderous roll that not only should have served to rouse the dead but also would have put a machine-gun battalion to shame.

There was one event that World's Fair summer, however, that

58

paid big dividends. And it was an artistic triumph as well. For some time past, André Kostelanetz had been following Lily Pons around, via air and otherwise, to pay court to the stunning and talented coloratura whom F.C. Coppicus had discovered and imported from France. Eventually he won out, they were joined in holy wedlock, and Coppicus offered them in joint appearances. Alert Minnie signed them up immediately.

When the night of July 17 arrived, the management was unprepared for what was to take place. Nothing like it had ever been seen before, nor has it since. At about 6:30 P.M. the stadium was filling up fast—so very fast that by 7:00 P.M. it was full, and it suddenly seemed that the whole city of New York must be converging on the stadium en masse.

It goes very hard when a ticket sale has to be stopped—especially when one has a seating capacity that had never in twenty-two years been fully tested at its maximum. Nevertheless, the order went out to all the cages through the intercommunicating system, all of which was simple enough. But getting the rest of the ticket holders in and keeping the other milling thousands out was not so simple. It was finally necessary to call on squads of police to assist in closing the five huge entrance gates. The final count was 20,475 admissions. Everything had conspired to make this a truly record-breaking occasion—the weather was perfect, the program was right, and the solo performers not only were in great form but also had demonstrated a record-breaking draw.

Probably the only occasion when a stadium concert was not given in the Lewisohn Stadium itself was one evening in July of 1941. Robert Moses, New York Park Commissioner, had finally persuaded Mrs. Guggenheimer to try out the Marine Amphitheater in Flushing Meadow Park. It will be recalled that this represented New York State's gift to the New York World's Fair. During the fair it had been the home of Billy Rose's famous Aquacade. It was a perfect starlit evening, and a charming program was given to about one-half a house and total receipts of only $1,534. The Aquacade was a white elephant, and a multimillion-dollar taxpayer investment never realized the purpose for which it was intended.

As the pioneer summer concert venture in this country, the

Lewisohn Stadium concerts persisted alone through many summer seasons until other cities acquired the courage to launch similar enterprises. On the West Coast rhe Hollywood Bowl concerts have achieved outstanding success as well as the Municipal Opera seasons in St. Louis and the Starlight Theater in Kansas City. More recently there have been launched the Garden State Center in Holmdell, New Jersey; Wolf Trap Farm in Washington, D.C.; the Blossom Center near Cleveland; and others, not to overlook the successful Tanglewood Concerts in the Berkshires.

9

Touring in Wartime— 1942-1943

"One-night stands are the best audiences in America. I never minded the physical effort of traveling."
—Ethel Barrymore

It was in mid-wartime during the winter season of 1942–1943 that Sigmund Romberg chose to launch a tour as conductor with his own orchestra—a secret ambition nourished by many composers and realized by only a few. After all, what is more logical than that the composer interpret his own works?

My services were acquired as business manager for the enterprise, and I accompanied the troupe to every engagement. Little did anyone dream, however, of the harrowing experiences that lay ahead in fulfilling a lengthy touring schedule under wartime conditions. Fortunately for the troupe and its ultimate success, Rommy turned out to be an inspiring and determined leader, as well as "a jolly good fellow."

The tour proved to be a saga of the road in wartime that was unmatched by any other company of fifty-odd players—every engagement was delivered, almost every one on time and without postponements. It was a saga replete with hectic experiences and sharp contrasts—high rewards as well as keen disappointments—but all capped with a sense of achievement. It was a pioneering job that was to pay big dividends in future seasons. Near the end of the record-making tour, railroad officials expressed amazement that the company could have been on the road all season and still be filling engagements on schedule.

The closest call Rommy and his company had in all 136 one-night stands during a sojourn of nearly six months on the road was an evening in early March of 1943. Tough as the schedule was, it was the avowed purpose to deliver every date, and on time, if humanly possible. On this particular evening the train pulled into the Oklahoma City station hours late, leaving less than half an hour to get on stage by curtain time. By 8:30 P.M., however, everyone was on hand in his seat ready for the opening beat. Few had eaten, but everyone had shaved (the ladies powdered), dressed, and spruced up; and edgy tempers had become pretty well smoothed over. All, that is, except for the tenor soloist, who was always avid for the best hotel room, the best seat on the train or bus, special accommodations, etc. Eventually his services were dispensed with and a new singer engaged. Everyone in the outfit was expendable, except Rommy himself.

The auditorium that night was cold and drafty, and the long train ride from Amarillo, Texas, in overheated cars had been unusually tiring. Nevertheless, a sprightly performance was turned in, which resulted in the usual rave notices from the press on the following day. And so the sixty-first concert of his own orchestra under the leadership of Sigmund Romberg had become history. Many performances were still in the offing, however, before *finis* was to be written to an extraordinary concert tour.

By 11:30 P.M. the entire troupe had boarded the Santa Fe Railroad train for its appearance the next evening in Dallas. That ride will always be a blessed memory—it was the first time in months of travel that the entire company had been able to secure sleeping space while traveling at night. Pullman accommodations were always at a premium because of army needs, but night travel was occasionally necessary to make the long jumps set by the booking office. After all, these were one-night stands, trains were usually late, and the next city was sometimes hundreds of miles away.

When I set out with Sigmund Romberg and his orchestra from New York the night before Christmas, there were only about three weeks of bookings ahead. With a carload of personnel and sixteen cases of instruments in the baggage car, as well as plenty of unsolicited warnings about wartime travel, it seemed a foolhardy enterprise. That night it stormed, and the next day the train plowed through heavy snow in the mountains of western Pennsylvania. Nevertheless, Pittsburgh was reached and concerts played on Christmas Day and the following evening with a success that seemed auspicious indeed for the hopes that had been placed in the venture. It was Rommy's theory that the public wanted his kind of music right at this time; he recalled vividly that that was their state of mind in 1917.

The company entrained that Saturday night out of Pittsburgh for Buffalo just in time, for the snow had turned to heavy rain, and the first of a series of floods was already on the way. Two days later, while the floods were at their worst, the troupe was in the far upper end of New York State, playing Rochester, Syracuse, and other cities. A week later, however, they were again back in flood territory—traveling from Columbus, Ohio, to Charleston, West Virginia, on the first train to go through in several days.

Again, in late March, the company went from Jackson, Tennessee, to Hattiesburg, Mississippi, on the first train through after a terrific storm had washed out a bridge and considerable trackage. Only the night before they were assured that it would be impossible to make Hattiesburg in time. But fate was pushing Rommy and his troupe along to make all those engagements.

A few days later they were to play in Evansville, Indiana, with Ohio River floodwaters still at their peak. Evansville had been previously played on February 7, when the crest of the earlier flood was at its height. This time it seemed as though the water was about to reach the street level in front of the McCurdy Hotel, but it began to lose height that same night. This ex-

63

perience was particularly harrowing, for we had reached Nashville at about 7:30 A.M. after the performance in Jackson the night before, in order to connect with the train for Evansville. The company was just ten minutes short of making the connection, although they had wired ahead and been assured that the train would be held. With no other trains out during the day and Evansville 161 miles away and much baggage to be moved, as well as the company, prospects looked bleak for the concert that night.

Adequate bus accommodations were finally arranged and a truck located to haul the baggage. Then, the crux of the situation came about ten miles out of Evansville when we neared the flooded zone. For several miles floodwaters had reached both sides of the road but were never quite high enough to stop traffic from getting through. It was an immense relief to finally get across the Ohio River at Henderson, Kentucky, where the water was all of ten feet above flood level.

The next morning the move out of Evansville was in another heavy downpour. "Romberg rides again" was echoed by fifty relieved voices as our train finally pulled out of the station only two hours late.

Lest the impression is given that the only kind of adverse weather was wet, it should be added that blizzards as well as hot and cold extremes of temperature were also encountered. Strange as it may seem, almost springlike weather in Winnipeg, Canada, in the middle of February was to be followed two weeks later by bitter cold and a genuine Rocky Mountain blizzard at Colorado Springs. A temperature of thirty below at Grand Forks, North Dakota, was to be contrasted with summer weather in New Orleans and heat of 100° F in Charlotte and Winston-Salem, North Carolina, at the end of May.

Weather hazards, however, serious as they are in trouping, were surely exceeded in wartime by transportation and hotel difficulties. The manager would rather combat the elements any time than have to announce to his troupe in the lobby of the town's principal hotel that they had no sleeping accommodations for that night. Then, perhaps, he had to tell them the next morning at the railroad station that the coach which the railroad was placing at their disposal for the day's jump had just been requisitioned by the army. And very likely the only choice then left was for the company to stand up or, sometimes, to divide up between two or three trains, or secure transportation by bus.

One of the manager's duties is to provide hotel accommodations for the company. But in wartime it was difficult enough to assemble a first-rate group of musicians who would consent to the arduous conditions of daily travel, so everything had to be done to assure a minimum of comfort. And, even though accommodations arranged for in advance were generally available, there were always those who preferred to go elsewhere. One group in particular—they were dubbed the "Delta Rhythm Boys"—always disappeared somewhere as soon as they hit a town. It was rumored that they had their own method of holing in somewhere at something like one dollar per head per night, but the details were never quite clear. In any case, they were always on hand at concert time.

The William Morris Agency booked the attraction not only in legitimate concert halls and theaters but also in arenas and gymnasiums—almost every type of covered building that had seating capacity. Probably the oddest spot of all was the Corn Palace in Mitchell, South Dakota. This was a lonesome spot—one of those places that, as soon as you get into, you realize a mistake has been made and cannot get out fast enough. You can always feel out the atmosphere of a place by the time you have arrived at the hotel. Although this was a small town (about 20,000 population), nobody seemed to have heard of the concert, and Rommy wondered whether it had been promoted.

It was only after some telephoning around that I was able to locate the sponsor, who said there didn't seem to be much interest in the event; he knew little about the advance sale (thought possibly 400 tickets had been sold), and finally he said he figured that people would be buying tickets at the door that night. In fact, it was soon apparent that the whole affair was pretty much of an imposition on that gentleman's time and disposition. Rommy's first reaction was to move right on to St. Paul and better things. On second thought, however, he decided to stick it out and give them all he had.

Capable of seating about 4,000 persons, the Corn Palace itself was a huge bare barn of a hall where exhibitions were held. The outside walls of the structure were completely covered with huge patterns and designs formed by attaching thousands of ears of multicolored ears of corn against the sides of the building. In any event, Rommy gave the prairie gentry the best program he knew how, and the enthusiasm more than made up for the meager size of the audience.

At this point the experience on the next night should also be mentioned. The town played was Vermillion, South Dakota, where our troupe was the first to appear there since John Philip Sousa and his band played some of the whistle-stops many, many years before. In getting off at the modest but well-kept station, all we could see was a farmhouse or two. With baggage and instruments stacked on the station platform and most of the company sitting around, I set out to secure transportation to the auditorium. First, it was necessary to find the town. This was located on a high bluff behind the station, and, since taxis were apparently nonexistent, everyone trekked to the auditorium. Rommy and the soloists put up at the Waldorf Hotel— meals were forty cents, and there were no keys to the rooms.

When contact was finally made with the sponsors, they were found to be most charming and hospitable. No one could ever forget the wonderful Sunday night supper of delicious waffles and ice cream which had been arranged at a private home. Cream, eggs, and butter were used without stint—a heart-warming contrast to the usual hotel and train fare.

It came as a surprise to discover a fine, modern, well-equipped, and well-managed auditorium located on the grounds of the University of South Dakota. The capacity was about fourteen hundred persons, which must have been about one-half the entire local population. Although the attendance was fairly good, the "take" just about covered the bus fare out of town. Accommodations (the Waldorf Hotel could take care of only twelve persons) being on the short side and train service infrequent, I finally secured two buses and moved the company on to Yankton after the performance. The Yankton Hotel (dating from the 1870s) was a hostelry left over from frontier days and prided itself on once having been host to Buffalo Bill in his scouting days. So, accordingly, everyone set to wondering who would draw the famed frontiersman's room. At 2:00 A.M., however, no one really cared much, so the matter never was settled.

Several towns were played in the Dakotas, but, though the people were cordial and very friendly, the endless miles of bleak snow-covered prairie at twenty to thirty degrees below zero were not conducive to good spirits. No one will ever forget the early-morning hours spent at Glyndon Junction, Minnesota, en route from Fargo to Winnipeg. At 11:45 P.M. after the concert at the former city, the whole troupe was hustled to the station and entrained to this forsaken spot where it was necessary to change trains to the main line going into Canada. Inasmuch as the next train was over three hours in arrears, there was a chilly wait ahead.

So the company divided itself between a two-by-four shack (said to be the station house) and an old railroad car with a wood stove in one end, which the railroad company had thoughtfully moved onto a siding for the "comfort" of the company. In my state of mind, it was impossible to catch any sleep, so I indulged in the periodic recreation of going out and peering through the below-zero night, trying to catch a glimpse of the headlights of the train supposed to be coming up from the south. The principal recompense, however, was a gorgeous and awe-inspiring display of the northern lights.

Then there were still the border formalities to go through. Canada was necessarily being very technical in wartime, and all instruments and luggage were given a thorough going-over. Manifests and all necessary papers had been prepared in advance, so fortunately there were no complications to cause further delays. The concert in Winnipeg was one of the most successful of the tour.

It was still below zero when we reached the Twin Cities, where a huge sold-out house of twelve thousand persons in St. Paul was most inspiring—quite a contrast to the lean days in the Dakotas. As the treasury suddenly took a turn for the better, so did everything else; and the company began working its way down through the Middle West with New Orleans and sunshine the goal a month hence. While the company had all along remained in blissful ignorance, the ways and means committee (consisting of maestro and manager) had met and survived its first, last, and only serious financial crisis. It was now possible each week to send remittances back to the bank in New York.

Rommy was ever cheerful and confident. A born raconteur with a colorful background of rich experience, he could always produce new and delightful stories during low moments, such as the sojourn at Glyndon. Very seldom out of sorts, he was always democratic and an excellent trouper while maintaining a proper relationship with his musicians. All his songs have been written incidental to his shows, of which he composed over seventy. These have included the well-known *Desert Song*, *Maytime*, *Student Prince*, *New Moon*, *Blossom Time*, *My Maryland*, and *Up in Central Park*.

In an interview in the Winnipeg *Tribune*, Rommy was quoted as declaring that "music has no future unless it has a melody. When people remember Ravel's Bolero, they don't beat out the rhythm of the drums, they hum the melody." Frequently asked which of his many songs was the favorite, his reply was, "When I Grow Too Old to Dream."

Romberg could always draw inspiration for another song from "a lad and a lassie in the moonlight," but he seemed never to be moved by the majesty of nature. I well remember standing on the railroad platform at Colorado Springs, waiting for the train out to Pueblo. It was the morning after a severe blizzard. The giant snow-covered Rockies, dominated by Pike's Peak, were ranged against the dazzling blue of the western sky, and on every side the fresh blanket of snow glistened under a dazzling sun. I offered a comment on the beauties of nature but only got a nod from Rommy. En route, he appeared to ignore the landscape almost entirely, usually discussing program or personnel problems with Eddie Rubsam, his contractor; discussing other problems and plans with me; sometimes catching catnaps; or playing gin rummy.

Born in Hungary, Sigmund Romberg spent much of his youth in Vienna. There he received his university training and learned to play the violin, cello, trumpet, tympani, organ, and piano. There also he met Franz Lehar and other leading spirits of the gay, musical Vienna that was. Doubtless the influence of this happy, carefree background had a hand in forming the modern, jovial Bohemian character who became such a prolific composer of show music. He loved choice food at the best restaurants; could pick up and play a violin on the station platform at Crestline, Ohio, and make the company forget its griping; and could regale the hostess and her select company at the piano with no end of witty stories.

Rommy was very much a prankster, and one of his best stories revealed a streak of devilry that not even sedate London society could squelch. The most successful of his shows abroad was *The Desert Song*, produced at the famed Drury Lane Theatre, where it ran for two years. It seems that the so-called dress rehearsal was customarily a preview, attended principally by the lords of the realm and their ladies in full-dress regalia. For all practical purposes it was what we in America would know as an opening night.

All went smoothly and beautifully until the opening of the third act. The overture was finished and action on stage begun when the leading man missed a piece of business. Instead of passing over the situation and making the correction later, Rommy stopped the music (he was conducting) and put the unfortunate performer through his paces on the spot. After all, it was supposed to be a dress rehearsal. But, of course, it was a shocking breach of etiquette. One of the peers sought out Rommy later in his dressing room to congratulate him on the splendid performance—particularly the interruption which he and his party had accepted as highly amusing.

As a personality, Sigmund Romberg was almost unknown to the country at large, hence the tour proved a revelation. Although not a Toscanini with the baton, he had an inimitable manner all his own that quickly endeared him to audiences everywhere. In one place a lady admirer of his music even commented that she had thought Romberg was dead. Such a possibility could be understood, for much of his music had already become a lengendary part of American show literature, along with that of Victor Herbert and a few others.

At his home in Beverly Hills, California, Romberg had assembled one of the world's finest operatic libraries. The several hundred items—many of great value—included complete sets of everything written by Victor Herbert, Reginald de Koven, and Giuseppe Verdi. Several of the scores have never had public performance.

Romberg was anything but an orthodox conductor. He even seated his musicians differently and placed the podium at one corner of the stage. In this way the audience at least had the advantage of watching him in profile, and it was easy for him to get over occasional asides to them. When introducing Marie Nash, an attractive soprano soloist, his inevitable remark, "I know a good voice when I see one," never failed to make a hit.

10

Romberg Rides Again

> "It is a great strain to
> conquer the hearts and
> feelings of thousands of
> persons every time one
> plays and yet, if the urge
> to do so is present, there is
> no happiness in doing
> anything else."
> —Mischa Elman

Whenever the Romberg troupe was finally entrained and about to roll again, there was a more and more familiar shout to be heard echoing through the cars: "Romberg rides again." Toward the end of the tour on the last lap homeward, in fact, this slogan could be heard daily every time the company set out for the next performance.

Box-office settlements ran the gamut from the sublime to the ridiculous—everything from the sponsored engagement where a flat fee was collected to the percentage deal with a green local manager. In Augusta, Georgia, there were tickets still out on consignment with various committees that had not yet been turned in for an accounting at the time of the concert. In another city the manager had had no prices printed on the tickets—he merely filled in the prices in ink according to what he thought the traffic would bear. There was no alternative but to figure the settlement from the amount of cash the manager said he had collected, certainly unorthodox procedure.

No one could possibly have anticipated some of the hazards on a new tour arranged by a new booker sitting in a New York office quite unconscious of the realities of wartime travel.

The best engagements were with the legitimate established local concert managers whose names I had given to the booking office early in the season. Such managers as J. Herman Thuman of Cincinnati, Marvin MacDonald of Atlanta, Arthur Oberfelder of Denver, Michaux Moody of Richmond, Arthur See of Rochester, and Chester Anderson of Dayton proved the best sponsors. Some others included fight promoters, committees of this and that, movie-house operators, colleges, and occasionally just anybody who would hire a hall and sign a contract.

Three times during the tour the company was routed back to New York for a brief but badly needed rest and to recuperate for the next session of hotel and train fare. Each time, however, the going became easier, and hardships lessened. Except for the prima donna tenor, soloists remained the same throughout the season. The malcontents and those who hit the wrong notes too often were weeded out until eventually a good ensemble resulted. From time to time, however, it was necessary to leave someone hospitalized behind and have a substitute sent on from New York. And occasionally one of the younger musicians would ruefully come around with the draft notice he just received from home.

In spite of the strenuous conditions, there was very little illness. The company played in drafty halls, rehearsed in their overcoats, got in and out of hot trains, and generally were exposed to the elements in all their extremes. And, during all the season's traveling, only once did one musician oversleep and miss the train call. He was several days catching up. At first Rommy intended to dock him, but the man was so terribly embarrassed that nothing was said.

As the tour prospered, help was acquired. Originally, I was not only business and tour manager, but stage manager, electrician, baggage man, and even secretary to the maestro himself. Eventually the added personnel included one person for each of these four functions. Everyone worked out well, except the baggage man. At each stop he got drunker and still

72

drunker until finally he was put on a train headed back to New York.

The company always arrived at its destination, but sometimes the baggage did not. The best policy was usually to ship it out on the first possible train after a concert. Once in Philadelphia I took the company off at the Broad Street Station while the baggage was inadvertently put off at another station. Although the concert was on the same evening, it seemed like hours before the luggage could be located; each station, in the meantime, claimed it did not have any of the baggage.

The worst miscarriage took place at White River Junction in New Hampshire. The troupe was traveling on a Sunday from Montreal, Canada, to Springfield, Massachusetts. In some still unaccountable manner, in switching railroads at this junction point the baggage car was left behind. The shock came, however, on arrival at Springfield late in the day. Running down the whereabouts of the baggage took time; then came the question of how to replace double basses, a harp, tympani, etc., on a Sunday in a small city. After running down every possibility, I finally persuaded the high school music instructor to loan instruments from the school orchestra after giving him the custody of one thousand dollars cash to hold as security.

There is one more baggage story. Early April of 1943 found the company in Akron, Ohio, the rubber city. In order to play Washington the following night, company and baggage had to be on hand at the station before 5:30 A.M. the following day to board the Shenandoah, the fast, streamlined train that would reach the nation's capital just in time for this most important concert. There was no baggage car on the train, only a very small compartment in the end of one of the cars. After bribing the baggage man, who wanted to leave everything, it was possible to just squeeze in the tympani, one bass, and the smaller pieces. This left the other bass and harp, which the conductor refused to carry. Artists, however, always want their own instruments, and many cities remained to be played at distant points to which these two pieces would never catch up were they left behind.

Another handout and the conductor relented. The harp was stood up in the vestibule of one coach, and the bass was laid on

73

its side (it was in a hard case) in the passageway between two cars. All day long people had to stumble over this instrument in going from one car to the next. Although it was against all the rules, it had to be charged up to one more wartime emergency that abrogated many ordinary procedures.

Arrival in Washington was just about in time to prepare for and play the concert in Constitution Hall. But the hotel reservations had been lost in the meantime, so everyone had to move right out and on to Philadelphia the same night. Even though I had called ahead for reservations, they did not exist on arrival in the City of Brotherly Love in the very early-morning hours. Some of the players remained to sleep in the Statler lobby; a few managed to secure rooms; some got their rooms later in the morning as guests checked out, and others wandered out into the night.

Rommy and company were still not through with Akron, however. They were to return three weeks later to take care of those who had been unable to get in to the first concert there. And again there was a near tragedy at train time. One of the soloists, in a fit of temperament over an imagined wrong, had worked herself into a hysterical state. She was all for going right back to good old New York on the next train. No one could calm her or persuade or reason with her in any way. A musician could be missed now and then, but all the soloists were essential. Everyone was on the train, and "All aboard!" was being called out when I picked up her one hundred pounds and hustled her aboard. The scene was finished en route, but she sang in the next concert.

In traveling, the company naturally broke up into groups and cliques. Some amused themselves on the trains with poker or gin rummy; others read or studied; and many slept. They never had enough sleep. Ralph Singer, stage manager and one-time actor, never failed to bring the house down with his impersonations of some of the musicians. The first time these were sprung quite by surprise. He must have been rehearsing for some time in private, as they were too well-polished to have been impromptu. In any case, someone knew about them and unexpectedly called on him in the course of one of those long dull train jumps. He brought down the house, especially when

74

conducting a la Romberg. The act took so well that the repertoire was augmented on subsequent occasions and presented whenever the company was lucky enough to have a railroad car to themselves.

One of the early malcontents among the orchestra personnel was the heavy, thick-set alien who carried the little AFM. green book of rules, etc., in his vest pocket and was always checking up the manager and wiring Petrillo's office. He objected to traveling over three hundred miles per day, would not accept his pay with the taxes taken out, wanted extra money for traveling at night, etc. He would get the company stirred up, and meetings would be held to air grievances—imagined and otherwise. On returning to home base in New York for the first stopover, his name was promptly removed from the roster.

Wedged into an already crowded schedule (bookings were so close there was scarcely a night off) were appearances at various training camps and service hospitals. At Fort Knox, Kentucky, Rommy played the field house in the afternoon and the auditorium in Louisville the same night.

At Kansas City, Air Force bombers were on hand to take the company to an aviation training center at Sedalia, then back for the evening concert. At Wright Field, near Dayton, a thrilling concert was played in one of the hangars. Incidentally, Dayton will always occupy an especially soft spot in everyone's memory. They really liked the performance. After playing the city's auditorium on Saturday evening, January 9, a return engagement was played two days later and also sold out. Then a third sold-out concert followed in the spring on the third of April.

After our traveling up and down and across the Middle West a number of times that season, it seemed to us as if the whole Mississippi River Valley had been turned into a gigantic armed camp. Almost everywhere there was a special training camp of some kind. Radio experts were being turned out by the hundreds weekly at Sioux Falls, Iowa; at Denver chemical warfare officers were just completing the world's largest poison-gas arsenal nearby; at Chattanooga and Des Moines the WACs were entertained. Miles of war factories, storage depots, bases, and fields were passed; more than once the train was held on a siding while long trains of war supplies and troops had the right of way; highways were choked with movements of troops either on maneuvers or concentrating for embarkation; in short, on every side was evidence of vast preparations for the war being fought on far-flung global fronts.

In Evansville, Indiana, nothing could be found to eat after the concert on a Sunday evening. It seemed that the thousands of soldiers on weekend leave from a nearby camp had actually eaten the town out. Artists frequently eat their biggest meals after a performance, so it was tough to have to forego the usual steaks and beer. Rommy, however, took it all in good stride and was uncomplaining.

On the night jumps I was generally able to secure drawing room or Pullman space of some kind for Rommy and, usually, the soloists. On three occasions when trains were boarded late at night, the maestro's space was already taken — it had been sold twice. Going out of Pueblo, Colorado, at midnight, bound for Amarillo, Rommy's drawing room proved to be non-existent. Mrs. Romberg had recently joined her husband and had been taken ill. A helpful conductor, however, found other space, and one more problem was left behind.

Time and space preclude mention of a host of other occurrences that lent spice to daily travels — some depressing, some humorous, and some inspiring. There was the sad moment when cellist Antosch tripped on a carpet going into the Rice Hotel in Houston and practically put one foot through the side of his beautiful, carefully polished instrument. In addition to being a first-rate musician, Albin Antosch was a self-effacing gentleman who never made trouble of any kind and was always on the job. And no one could possibly have treasured more or taken better care of his instrument. Somehow he managed to make temporary repairs and continued playing as usual.

Then there was the time when the Maple Leaf Gardens in Toronto was played — an important engagement, for the place seated more than ten thousand persons. At about five o'clock I had to get the doctor for one of the soloists. But I was assured she would sing. At about nine o'clock, shortly before her first stint on the program, I was advised there would be no singer that night. So an appropriate announcement had to be made and the program numbers quickly reshuffled. She was left in the hospital to recover and catch up with us several days later.

At Steubenville, Ohio, (Stupidville, some called it) Eddie Rubsam slipped in the tub during his shower and suffered a gash on his head that required several stitches. But he played that night as usual.

Ordinarily, the rule was to eat, drink, and get to bed after a concert, for who could tell what the morrow would bring? Inevitably more travel, another insulting hotel, and, of course, a concert. And, even though the booking office had not succeeded in making all the jumps as complicated and as far distant as possible, it was still good policy to get on the move early. Inadvertently, a few of the jumps turned out to be easy and short. So then the troupe would have a chance to look around or get additional rest while the manager tried to remember for the record what he had expended several days back; to check up on the local situation to see if there would be a good house that night; and then to wrestle with new transportation and hotel problems.

While travel was uncertain and hazardous enough, I always felt that a good 90 percent of the railroad officials were earnestly trying to cooperate in every reasonable way to expedite travel. Some hotels were certainly high-handed and took much less interest in the proceedings. Fifty people dropping in for overnight were unwanted guests, especially on weekends. On the whole, the company was patient and understanding, but there were always the inevitable prima donnas. Some of them could not sleep in double rooms; some had to be on the rear side of the hotel away from street noises; some were too price conscious and hotels would not bargain; and some had to be high up off the street.

In Savannah, almost no reservations were available. I happened to have a large corner room and took in as many of the musicians as possible. Others slept in the park just across the street. The boys could be seen stripped to their shorts (it was very hot) lying on the grass and benches. In Dayton, the Biltmore turned over the ballroom to the company. This arrangement led to so much friction and griping that thereafter I put the company up in Cincinnati and made special trips back

77

and forth to fill the four engagements in Springfield and Dayton. Of course, there were some hotels who remembered what touring companies had meant to them in other days and tried to retain goodwill for a possible future occasion.

While on the home stretch a second engagement was filled in Columbus, Ohio. Mail there included a letter (fortunately not too important) that had been sent to the manager for the first concert four months earlier. Someone was either too dumb to bother forwarding the communication or else had a premonition that he would be back later.

On the first visit when checking in at the Deshler-Wallick Hotel a sumptuous suite was placed at Rommy's disposal gratis. It turned out that Mr. Wallick had not forgotten the occasion a quarter of a century earlier when the maestro had gotten up a floor show for him (while he was manager at Claridge's in New York) that turned a losing eating place into a winner.

As Rommy entered the hotel's dining room for refreshment and sustenance after the concert, the house orchestra shortly went into a succession of Romberg tunes. When the maestro became recognized, guests at other tables began moving closer. Then Rommy ordered the tables put together in banquet fashion—everyone was to eat and drink as his guests. He then got into one of his story-telling moods, and a gala time was had by everyone—much more fun than the formal concert. On a few occasions this scene was to be repeated in other cities, sometimes at private homes.

Occasionally there were invitations that could not be refused for after-concert parties. The private party usually meant two or three hours added to an overlong day, but the hosts were always charming and prominent and had gone to a great deal of trouble. After the first concert in Rochester there was a most delightful party at the home of one of the city's first citizens. The food was superb and the company fascinating, so Rommy was inspired to do some of his fables at the piano, and the raconteur in him kept everyone until a very late hour.

Then there should be mentioned the lavish reception in the sumptuous home of Morton May (department store magnate) near St. Louis. The Ridders in St. Paul were also most cordial and hospitable. Gus Sun, famed veteran Middle West vaudeville booker, entertained Rommy in his Springfield mansion. Isaac Meyer, art lover and music patron, had a reception for him in his beautifully appointed apartment in Memphis. And there were others equally worth mentioning, not to overlook the unique buffet supper given by Alfred G. Arvold in one of the rooms adjoining the Little Country Theater at North Dakota State College in Fargo.

No one was sorry when the party to end them all was given by Rommy himself for the company on the roof of the Robert E. Lee Hotel in Winston-Salem on the evening of Friday, June 4. There was only one concert to go to successfully conclude a momentous tour. There was plenty of beer and other liquids, an abundance of food, speeches, and wisecracks. The next morning "Romberg Rides Again" was heard in chorus throughout the company's car as the train pulled out for concert Number one-thirty-six in Roanoke that night.

Romberg and company had traveled approximately thirty-five thousand miles — mostly by train, sometimes by bus. Against a vast kaleidoscopic panorama of American landscapes and cities, all abnormally activated by wartime requirements, they had pushed their way and fulfilled every engagement. It was a nightmare of trains, restaurants, baggage, hotels, theaters, auditoriums, and taxis — all conspiring to tax human patience and endurance. But the troupe had had its moments, such as the ovation from the great audience in St. Paul after the lean prairie audiences of the Dakotas; the successive sellouts in several cities; and, of course, the knowledge that a new attraction had been successfully launched.

An extraordinary tour even in peacetime, it was fantastic under wartime conditions.

11

The Ridgeway Theater

> "The purpose of playing . . .
> was and is, to hold as
> 'twere the mirror up to
> nature; to show virtue her
> own feature, scorn her
> own image, and the very
> age and body of the time
> his form and pressure."
> —Shakespeare

Through four seasons and four dozen plays we derived the inevitable joys, disappointments, breaks, and financial deficits inherent in a summer-stock theater operation. The overall expenses added up to a grand total of close to thirty thousand dollars in excess of income during the summers of 1939–1942.

Although summer audiences are generally more tolerant, our productions were necessarily on a high level because we were catering to the sophisticates of the New York metropolitan area. It was this constant endeavor to maintain a high standard of production and to have each play pay for itself within the limited engagement of a week that made the summer theater operation a constant struggle to just break even.

Simultaneously with the consideration of each play one must also think practically about (1) who is available to play it well? (2) how large is the cast? (3) how many and how complicated are the sets? (4) is the budget within limits? and, finally, (5) does it fit in with the rest of the season being planned? There is, too, the unavoidable pitfall of the play that reads well but does not act well and vice versa. The telephoning involved is prodigious, and the interviews with actors are endless. Enthusiasm for the new season, however, lures one on, and eventually everything falls into place.

This love of the theater must be the motivating force to compensate for the long hours and the dedication required. You must be ready to seriously discuss the theater at breakfast, throughout the day, and over your midnight snack. But the commodity in which you deal is largely ideas—those of production—not to overlook promoting ticket sales.

The lists of plays produced on Broadway in recent years is one of the first sources considered by the summer producer and director. Then there are the lists of those available from the play publishing companies; new plays from friendly authors and agents; and one's private store of favorites.

Years ago, David Belasco said, "The producer's job is to translate moods and supply the medium by which they are transmitted to audiences." The audiences at our Ridgeway Theater totalled 150,000 people in four summers on the basis of a five-hundred-seating capacity. The staff for such a venture included the producer as general manager, a stage director, scene designer, stage manager, electrician, technician, property man, carpenter, two painters, and the stagehands. On the theater staff were press representative, subscription manager, two box-office treasurers, ticket takers, porters, ushers, and refreshment concessionaire.

Regardless of the size of the cast, condition of the weather, and first-night notices, salaries went on and on. Strange duties devolved upon amiable people, such as the actor who arrived from Cape Cod one morning after having driven all night with a shroud-like apparition in his car, which turned out to be Jane Cowl's hair dryer. We tried to joke with him about it, but his only response was: "Skip it, I've been cowled all week."

Nowhere in the theater today in this country does there exist a better training ground for talent than those summer seasons spent in a good repertory theater. In more recent years, the off-

Broadway theater has also provided many added opportunities for acting talent. Young actors do not always realize the value of the experience they are getting. The old troupers, however, value the opportunities for tackling new parts.

Frank Craven tried the "barn circuit" after fifty-seven years of acting and said, "I've done my share of trouping. I don't think there is a town of over five thousand that I've missed. I'm trying to catch up on some of the sleep I lost when I was a kid. It's too bad that kids can't troupe now. You met people, studied dialects. You got so you could tell a Georgian dialect from a Tennessee one and a Maine from a Massachusetts. I've never tried this summer theater thing before; but I got tired of doing the same thing."

Miriam Hopkins came to her summer stock appearances from many seasons in Hollywood, where she was known as one of the hardest workers on the West Coast. The temptation might well have been to treat it as a week's vacation, but the contrary was true, for her energy and endurance in long rehearsals outlasted everyone else's. No detail was unimportant, and her costumes were as perfect as if they were for a Broadway production—and they were paid for out of her own salary!

For trouping, however, no one could excel Ethel Barrymore. We worked with her under varying circumstances, and she always broke precedents successfully. In *Whiteoaks*, she sold out two rival theaters twenty miles apart within three weeks of each other and then returned to one of them two weeks later and played a part fifty years younger in *The Constant Wife*. Her poise could not be shaken by heat or disturbing incidents. She carried her own vacuum bottle of ice cubes and iced coffee, and never at any time did she ask for special service. On opening night of *Whiteoaks*, a big blue bottle fly lighted on her nose during the longest part of the first act as she sat facing the audience scolding her brood of offspring. Not by a flick of an eyelash did Miss Barrymore betray the presence of the fly, which paraded up and down the bridge of her nose for what seemed, from front-row seats, like an age.

Jane Cowl, in contrast, arrived accompanied by her maid, secretary, Liebchen (a dachshund), and an English bicycle (which she never rode). No amount of service was sufficient, but, nevertheless, a fine performance resulted. She, too, had an appreciation for certain values of summer stock. She once commented, "We do not play summer shows for money, even though we may be well paid. No money, really, could make up for what we all undergo during rehearsals in the heat. But the summer theater means that we are helping to stimulate interest in the winter theater, that we are keeping familiar theatergoers and breaking in new audiences."

Lovely Edith Atwater (*The Man Who Came to Dinner*, etc.) kept herself from being typed by trying various types of roles each year in summer stock. She said, "It tunes one up, makes one keener." Certainly it did in the season she played Gertrude in *Fashion* and sang several popular songs of the year 1845, including "Come, Birdie, Come." She was certain that she couldn't possibly do it and then never ceased being surprised at the encore the audience always demanded.

But first and last the play is the thing. Productions in a summer stock season seem to fall into three classes—revivals, new plays, and touring plays. The latter is classed separately, for the touring play is more often than not a vehicle for a star and must be booked as a package if you want the star. Most satisfactory from every artistic standpoint is the selection of a well-known, finely written play that has stood the test of many performances and that can be cast according to the producer's own choice and pocketbook. You do away with the idiosyncrasies of the reviewer, who cannot argue the merit of a play already proven, although, of course, he can demand a good production.

Of the many revivals produced, two were outstanding. First, Eugene O'Neill's *Emperor Jones*, for which Paul Robeson was induced to return from London after an absence of several years. The play itself is so good and Robeson's acting was so superb that the whole cast and staff were inspired to exceptional effort. Robeson had first won fame in this vehicle on Broadway in 1924, so the original director, Harold McGee, was secured. Asadata Dafora, an African dancer with a wide knowledge of voodoo rites, played the witch doctor; African drummers of the Mendi Tribe pounded out throbbing native rhythms. Scenic designer Larry Goldwasser created a forest scene of great imagination at nominal expense.

The entire production represented one of those rare experiences when everyone participating was inspired in his work, and the monetary result was just as rewarding. After having played to full houses all week, Paul Robeson gratefully returned his salary check to us as his contribution to the future of the Ridgeway Theater. The show was an immense success, and its reviews in the New York press were comparable to a Broadway opening.

The passing of Paul Robeson removed from our midst one of the last of a galaxy of great talents that dominated the performing arts during the first half of this century. Highly educated, his artistic capabilities gained for him top billing both in concert and on stage as an actor. In addition to all that he was a warm human being, possessed of immense personal charm.

Fashion, or *Life in New York*, one of America's earliest comedies, was written by Mrs. Anna Cora Mowatt in 1845. It was a pleasure to revive, though not so rewarding at the box office. Five sets taxed the scenic department. Special candle footlights were installed and a "full orchestra" of violin and harp was used. Costumes were an added expense; but to give the customers variety in a summer stock season as well as a change of pace for the staff, such a bill provides satisfaction in a well-rounded season.

The package touring plays offer certain special problems to a summer stock producer. Naturally, he likes to include the few available "name" stars in his season in order to please the audience and (he hopes) to make a profit to carry over the lean weeks. But this latter hope can become purely theoretical.

Ethel Barrymore played in *The Corn Is Green* through one summer season after she had finished it on Broadway. Naturally, she rehearsed it in early summer with the cast she wished to use in each theater. For her purpose it could not have been handled in any other way, for it was a difficult play to cast. Twenty-eight people (many of them from the original New York company) were paid far more than the usual stock fees, and the six regular equity actors hired for the season could do nothing but find ways to help on the production. With a weekly gross of $7,600, the cast, staff, royalty, and rent totalled $6,500, with sets duplicating the New York production still to be accounted for.

On the other hand there is the case of *Springtime for Henry*, with Edward Everett Horton—a perennial joy to the box office. One of the funniest plays of all time, it had more laughs than anyone could possibly anticipate in a single evening. And the box-office returns literally salvaged the 1939 season. After all, there were only four characters and one set; and every performance was SRO. It was fun enough just to watch Edward Everett from out front, but to see him from backstage several times in succession put on the famous double takes and create laughs in the same manner every day was even more delightful.

In any season, the most intriguing, disappointing, and exacting production is the new play. It is produced with one hope in the hearts of all concerned: that it is destined for Broadway and possibly Hollywood. Rarely does a phenomenal success turn up in this way. *Life* magazine summed up the situation tensely: "This summer 74 plays tried out for Broadway but according to the sad statistics of other years, only 6% will make it."

Of the Ridgeway Theater production of Ferenc Molnar's *The Guardsman*, Sidney Whipple wrote in the New York *Telegram*:

> The production is aided, moreover, by an exceptionally smart portrayal by Kent Smith of the husband of the tantalizing lady (Miriam Hopkins). Some time ago I remarked that many times (many critics who never go to a summer theater will be surprised to learn) you will find better acting on the straw hat circuit than on Broadway. Perhaps the absence of strain and the nervousness of first nights have something to do with it. The actors are relaxed and express greater individuality. They are not so much automatons. . . . *The Guardsman*, it might be added, is perfect summer theater fare since it demonstrates Molnar's self-avowed purpose in life which is to entertain people and not to bother them with problems they couldn't understand anyway.

We had our tryouts too! The first was a musical revue entitled *Two Weeks with Pay*. Assembled by Ted Fetter and Richard

Lewine from the songs and sketches of various name writers, it was an ambitious project for any summer theater anytime anywhere. The now-famous Gene Kelly directed the dances and had never even reached the yelling stage when he saw the dawn come up like thunder at the final dress rehearsal.

The best summary of this show was written by Sidney B. Whipple, in the New York *World Telegram:*

> There were three highlights in the entertainment: 1) the first was the satirical dancing of Ruth Mata and Eugene Hari; [then unknown and just arrived in this country] 2) the eccentric dancing of Melissa Mason; 3) a number called "Noises in the Street" with music by Richard Lewine and lyrics by Peter Barry and David Gregory. Anybody who has lived in New York and encountered doormen, ash can collectors and itinerant bassoon players making the night hideous will laugh himself into hysterics over this one.

Years later "Noises in the Street" came into its own and was the hit number of *Make Mine Manhattan.* In the meantime, it followed a devious road to success, for it spent one night on Broadway in *Tis of Thee;* it was dropped from *Star and Garter* before it reached the city; Hume Cronyn used it in a USO revue; and later it was on the rural circuit again!

New plays are unusually expensive to produce in summer stock. At one time we found ourselves rehearsing and paying for three casts a week for five weeks—119 actors on the payroll all at once. To any lover of the theater, however, the experience of taking a play from the author through its tryout production and finally to Broadway is an intriguing experience, as well as a peril.

Our production of *Village Green,* the first play by Carl Allensworth, should be considered here, for it was carefully planned and given every reasonable chance to prove itself worthy of living its life before Broadway audiences. Why it did not is anyone's guess!

Any theater project needs the enthusiasm and tireless energy of a director such as Felix Jacoves. His theater background was that of a hardworking craftsman, so when it was decided that *Village Green* was a worthwhile project, he never stopped thinking about it or working on it except from sheer exhaustion. Long-distance calls persuaded Frank Craven to come from Hollywood and rehearse for its opening in June, in order to have time for revisions before trying it out in Baltimore early in the fall.

The rest of the cast was carefully selected through many play readings, for all actors are eager at any time of the year to get into a new play that has a chance of a season on Broadway. Practically the whole cast stuck for the summer theater engagement, tryout, and three weeks on Broadway. *Variety* summed up the results of all the efforts. "*Village Green* is a homey, rustic comedy, light as thistledown, yet with sufficient punch to warrant a Broadway run. The comedy is sure-fire for pix, apparently being designed with some such idea in mind. . . . The play as it stands should have a long enough run to warrant a film purchase."

The play was never sold to films, though even Howard Barnes in the *Herald-Tribune* said, "Five will get you ten that it will blossom forth as a motion picture and that it will prosper at the box office." Although Frank Craven gave a most compelling performance, his voice was not as strong as it formerly had been, and the difficulty of hearing him became a problem. A charming performer he was to work with and a loss to the theater when he passed on.

Two other plays that eventually reached Broadway after being first produced at Ridgeway were *The Two Mrs. Carrolls* and *Kind Lady*. The former starred Elizabeth Bergner and had a great success— 955 performances. Grace George, in *Kind Lady*, (which was produced by her husband, William A. Brady) was also a success on Broadway.

As we look back on our summer stock experiences, we like to especially remember hiring the unknown Gregory Peck for fifty dollars a week and finally signing him for forty dollars for a bit part in *Captain Jinks of the Horse Marines*.

In the *New York Times* of August 11, 1940, Benjamin Welles wrote,

> To the Ridgeway in White Plains every week come the biggest names on Broadway—Tallulah Bankhead, Jane Cowl, Ethel

Barrymore, Grace George, and many others. They arrive in monster limousines followed by attendant schools of station wagons. And throughout the hullabaloo and bustle, and dynamics and temperament calmly moves the virtual schoolmistress of this strange academy, Dorothy Olney, proprietor and manager of the Ridgeway Summer Theatre. It is said that nothing before or since the hurricane of 1938 has really upset Mrs. Olney, and it seems quite possible.

The Ridgeway itself had been under varied and unsuccessful management until two years previously when Mrs. Olney took it over. It was not long in becoming a sort of Mecca for the county residents, a playhouse hidden away off on a winding road that curves through the hills of Westchester. There, the county folks repaired after dinner, paid a reasonable price and saw both stars and plays that would do credit to a major Broadway season.

Mrs. Olney herself admits that were it not for her intense emphasis on complete professionalism throughout the theater, her many years' experience in gauging audience tastes, and the staff of assistants she has engaged, the Ridgeway Theatre could never have achieved its reputation. . . .

Even to the stagehands, the set builders, the painters and the press agent, Mrs. Olney stuck to a totally professional approach. All are union members and all treat their jobs at Ridgeway with the same care and solicitude as if they were at the moment on the Main Stem. So mature an approach to the problem of Summer Theatre—proverbially the stepchild of the stage proper—would indicate either years of dramatic experience or a dramatic birthright.

Dorothy Olney likes show people. Imbued with a quiet Yankee sense of humor and a patience backed by years of experience, she finds a tremendous kick in the bustle that goes on around Ridgeway. Though the Theatre itself holds but 550 people, it is modern in every sense of the word. Between the theatre and her office in nearby White Plains, Mrs. Olney shuttles busily all day long. From 10:00 A.M. till midnight she is on the go, . . . "trying to give the public the very best we can," in her own words. . . .

This singleness of purpose is quite natural when it is remembered that stars are now receiving as much as $1,500 for a week's appearance at summer theatres. So large a sum is not quickly realized in a house holding 550 seats which sell for $2.20, $1.10 and 55¢. It means that infinite care must be taken not only in attracting drawing names to Ridgeway, but the vehicles in which these stars appear must, as well, be thoughtfully selected. Mrs. Olney has found out that Broadway "names," though, without popular plays will do but half the business expected and needed to break even. Thus, the hard business head must reign supreme in ordering the affairs of summer stock. Mrs. Olney could never be accused of leaping before she looked.

Thus was Dorothy Olney's ability as an executive producer evaluated in the metropolitan press. The prestige thereby gained by her Ridgeway Theater soon placed it in the forefront of similar summer enterprises.

12

It Might Have Been

*"I have spent thirty years
in show business and still
don't know all of the
answers, and still take
beatings with shows that
should actually be a
financial success."*
—Harry Peebles, Wichita

To provide continuity for the theater professional, producer, or presenter, his thinking must be at least a year ahead of realization. As a consequence he must have projects in reserve from which to draw as failures or disappointments take place. This is easier said than done, but some of them may be worth recording here.

It may well be that only one in ten, or perhaps twenty, projects ever materialize. In some manner each new idea, or plan, or script, has to be tested. Even then it may not pass the ultimate test—public approval. Whether or not it achieves the ultimate of critical or public acceptance, or both, there are still other contingencies.

There were, of course, bound to be the usual efforts to get a show on Broadway. During the four-year period when we operated a summer playhouse in Westchester, we developed out of the forty-four shows produced three attractions that had potentials for success in New York.

One of these was *Two Weeks with Pay*, a sprightly and entertaining revue somewhat on the order of *Lend An Ear*. But we were talked out of it by this and that "authority" until it was too late.

The tryout of a new comedy piece, *Village Green*, was so successful that we decided to take it into New York. The star was Frank Craven, performing in his first stage show since *Our Town*. It was a delightful, small-town comedy that could well have been successful on Broadway, except for bad timing.

During the tryout at Ridgeway Theater (described in chapter 11), former associates of Craven's in the persons of William A. Brady and John Golden took an unusual interest in proceedings and were free with sage advice. Among other things, they urged us, "You must be sure to be the first show to open on Broadway in the fall." So we went into rehearsal in a hot July, and in an even hotter August, Dorothy took the company down to Baltimore for a break-in week.

Out-of-town notices were sufficiently encouraging so that the producers brought the show into the Henry Miller Theater on the day after Labor Day. Business was only fair, and the tenor of the New York reviews was not much better, so the show never had a chance to catch on. Various cuts were made in the payroll, and other costs were adjusted so that the show could run three weeks and thus secure the movie rights.

Because of the threatening war situation, the whole Broadway season had been exceptionally slow in starting; in fact, the next show did not open until October. Subsequent experience would indicate that *Village Green* could at least have lasted out the first half of the season if it had been opened a month later.

Then there was *The Two Mrs. Carrolls*, which was tried out in our Scarsdale Theater in the summer of 1942. Regarding this one, we had great confidence. It had played successfully in England for two seasons. The book was good, and the cast was quite adequate, but the show had some shortcomings, and investors lacked enough incentive to book the production for New York.

We were losing so much money on our season as a whole because of gas rationing and the war situation that we could not hold on to the property. Eventually the property was bought by Dr. Czinner for Elizabeth Bergner. It proved to be her first successful vehicle in this country and had a long and prosperous run on Broadway.

Failure to get a production for *Laura*, by Vera Caspery, was a keen disappointment. Financing was arranged until a lawyer told his client the piece would never hold up, and we lost our major investor. Then the movies bought the script, and the successful screen production of *Laura* resulted. Eventually it did achieve a stage production, but the bloom was off, and the result was an anticlimax.

At the time that Charles Laughton and Paul Gregory were liquidating their association, I began concentrating on the development of ideas and properties that would enable their unique policy to continue. One that was to become a consuming interest with me was the story of Edwin Booth.

The idea came one day while talking to Tyrone Power regarding his next stage vehicle. He had an inherent love of the theater, with its "in-person" audiences. An outstanding virtuoso performer, Tyrone was not only handsome but possessed one of the most beautiful speaking voices in the theater. The challenge was there for the right proponent. Tyrone did not immediately react to the suggestion, for there was no script ready to be submitted.

After casting about for a suitable writer, I was referred to Milton Geiger, a reputed authority on the period and an expert researcher. He was contacted and found the subject an inspiration as well as a challenge. It was more than a year later, early in 1958, when a script was finally forthcoming. Tedious and overwritten, it was more than an hour too long. He was finally told that when the script was cleaned up and made structurally sound, and about four thousand words eliminated, a contract would be forthcoming.

My idea had been to create an episodic vehicle whereby the several tragedies in the personal life of Edwin Booth would be interwoven with his stage representations of those great characters of tragedy for which he had become world famous. It was admittedly a tough assignment. The material was there, but its treatment required more skill and understanding than the author brought to his task originally.

Eventually, the script was placed on the market, but the author did promise to notify me should a firm offer be received. To my surprise, I read in one of the trade papers not long after that the property was sold to José Ferrer — my first information that another deal was even in the offing. As producer-director-star performer, Ferrer then proceeded with an attitude toward the whole affair that was quite alien from the original concept. Ferrer not only lacked any resemblance to the great Booth, he so emasculated the property that it fell flat. Reviews were generally bad, and the production's life on Broadway was only too brief.

Then there was a promising new musical entitled *Willie Loved Everybody*, a first script by a pair of writers who had intrigued Elmer Bernstein into writing the score. There were auditions in Hollywood and in Ivy Larric's apartment in New York. Michael Gordon had expressed interest in directing the piece, and at a prolonged session in the Bernstein studio, attempts were earnestly made to iron out weaknesses in the script. The writers were obtuse to the point of refusing to change even a comma in their precious script. At about 4:00 A.M. I had had enough. The whole project thereby went down the drain, including a talented score by one of the most original and accomplished composers of our time, not to mention many thousands of dollars in front money and much time and effort put in by the would-be producers.

A revival of the old comedy *Lady Audley's Secret*, or *Who Pushed George*, starring Anna Russell, was one project that should not have been allowed to lapse. It needed a talented artistic director to pull the music and other elements together and make the thing jell. Sometimes frustration wins out over persistence, but there are other times when a little more of the latter would have gotten the property produced. It's a real chancy business under the most favorable circumstances; the wrong advice at a crucial time can write finis prematurely.

The G.B. eSsence of Women was a promising property that was conceived, researched, and produced by Dorothy Olney in association with Prof. Day Tuttle, an authority on Bernard Shaw. The title was derived from one of the playwright's own writings, and the piece had everything to do with Shaw's women. They ranged from Mrs. Warren to Cleopatra, Lady Cicely to Candida, and Eliza Doolittle to Joan of Arc. Juxtaposing these characters in an evening of selections from nine of Shaw's plays was an intriguing idea that came off very well, indeed, under Tuttle's adroit direction.

The attraction was produced and presented for the fiftieth anniversary event of the ANTA Matinee Series. Critical comment, for the most part, was more than favorable. The star of the cast was Violet Heming. It was a delightful company. The curator of the theater collection of the New York Public Library, George Freedley, wrote us that the play was "brilliantly conceived and brilliantly acted . . . an evening of pure delight."

Several attempts were made to translate this effort into a major production, but they were aborted, largely because of casting problems. Jennifer Jones had expressed interest in the piece, so Dorothy and I met with her and David O. Selznick in an endeavor to work out a deal, but the conditions proved to be too complicated.

13

The Viking

> *"The basis of all artistic genius lies in the power of conceiving humanity in a new and striking way, of putting a happy world of its own creation in place of the meaner world of our common days."*
> —Walter Pater

Somewhat past the time when many singing artists have customarily gone into retirement, Lauritz Melchior was embarking on a new career—becoming a popular movie star. And not because his great voice was going off pitch or creaking with the years. Someone had discovered he was an actor of many parts, besides Wagnerian, and looked good in Technicolor.

For a brief period in the 1940s, the movie moguls had a crush on leading Met opera singers. None of them survived the impact, however, and it remained for the lusty Dane to show that it could be done. Possessed of a remarkable combination of talents in the grand manner, Lauritz came back stronger than ever. A more personable, charming, lovable character never existed. His remarkable success has been eminently well deserved, based on a real zest for living.

Almost coincidental to the celebration of Lauritz's twenty years with the Metropolitan Opera Company, when he was hailed as the world's leading interpreter of heroic tenor roles, came the release of his first picture, *Thrill of a Romance*. It opened up new horizons for his fabulous art. Just as he was a worthwhile addition to the roster of new film discoveries, so were the films a boon to the singing actor's popularity. Always making a good income as a concert and opera singer, it is estimated that his earnings were increased ten times.

Money restrictions, therefore, not being what they had been, the Heldentenor decided early in 1946 to henceforth concertize with orchestra accompaniment instead of the usual pianist. With bookings arranged by his business manager, James A. Davidson, I was appointed to handle the concert tours. They were compact schedules of only a few weeks at a stretch—quite in contrast to the hectic bookings of the Romberg tours. This business will always have its hectic aspect, but at least the degree of confusion can be reduced by better planning and more professional execution. The result is also a reduction in the hazards and "incidents," of which the reader obtained a sampling in the Romberg account.

Ordinarily an orchestra of forty pieces would be assembled in New York by George Weigl—violinist, contractor, and wit extraordinary. Then a set program would be thoroughly rehearsed. Then I would take the company out by chartered bus to the first city on the itinerary. The Melchiors would generally leave later and fly (how they love to fly) to this point. In the case of the first tour with orchestra this happened to be Columbia, South Carolina.

Here, at the very outset, trouble reared its ugly head. Most of the instruments were carried in luggage compartments on the huge bus, but it was necessary to ship the tympani separately, and they had not arrived. Music stores, schools, colleges, teachers, and every possible source in Columbia as well as in surrounding towns as far away as a hundred miles were canvassed in an effort to locate these two instruments. Strangely enough, no tympani could be located in the entire area, so it became necessary to get the percussion effects in another way.

The new type of Melchior recital proved an instantaneous success, and thereafter almost every concert was a sellout.

Physically of large stature and generously proportioned, Melchior and the effect of his rich tenor voice against the orchestral background were electrifying. No other singer had gone to the same trouble or expense. The public response was amazing. There was one week that Melchior sang eight times, receiving close to twenty-five thousand dollars as his share of the receipts—big money at that time.

The program material had a wide range of appeal. Primarily classical, the numbers included folk songs (Scandinavian), opera arias, and concluded with selections from Lauritz's various motion pictures. It was balanced fare and always satisfied. And it never failed to be a source of gratification that his efforts were helping substantially to spread a love for good music. He would be greeted backstage later not only by the usual bejeweled dowagers but by bobby-soxers in profusion as well. And he was perfectly at home with both, which, perhaps, helped to explain his amazing picture success.

Having a many-faceted talent had meant that Lauritz was under continual pressure from concert managers, movie producers, and the radio, as well as the Metropolitan Opera. Concert tours, therefore, had to be well organized and sandwiched in between other commitments. In order to cover distances and book as many concerts as possible into a month's time, it was decided to use planes in the late fall of 1946. Engagements were booked up and down the Pacific Coast from Vancouver to San Diego.

The best-laid plans oft can go awry, particularly in show business. This turned out to be such an extraordinary operation that it is worth recounting in more than the usual detail. It was the use of airplanes to cover the vast distances between cities that introduced an unusual element of hazard to this tour. But all the distances were covered, and all the bookings played, although not always on the dot of curtain time at 8:30 P.M.

A few days ahead of the opening date in Oakland, California, I was notified to the effect that no orchestra was available. Although an orchestra was an added luxury in the case of Melchior concerts, nevertheless, it was specified in the contracts, so an orchestra there had to be. It seems that the musicians who had been engaged by a contractor in San Francisco discovered that planes were to be used for travel and refused to fly. The musicians knew what Melchior did not—that the Pacific Northwest is subject to storms in November and, according to the little green book, they could not be made to fly their engagements. Nevertheless, an expensive contract had been signed with the Flying Tiger Line for two of its large transport planes. And, as has been stated, the Melchiors loved to fly.

Without going into all the details and a maze of figures, it turned out that three separate orchestras had to be employed. The original group from the San Francisco Symphony played the opening concert of the tour at Oakland. Then a hard-working contractor got together forty members from what had once been the Portland Symphony, and the rest of the northern dates were performed with them. For the southern dates a third orchestra was recruited from Hollywood. It all meant more rehearsing for Lauritz and the conductor, Otto Seyfert, but there was a considerable saving on travel expense.

The second date was to have been at Eugene, Oregon, where the Melchiors were to meet the musicians from Portland. Otto and I left San Francisco early in the morning by plane (the last to get off from the Municipal Airport that day) and were reveling in the vast panoramas of ocean and mountains meeting in a seemingly endless unbroken coastline when suddenly everything became white. All that could be seen for a distance of a few feet were the thick flurries of snow being blown against the wings of the plane. It had been plunged suddenly into a no-man's-land of sheer whiteness. For two hours—it seemed like two days—the plane continued north against head winds until, nearing Portland, the pilots were notified it would be impossible to land in the storm. So they turned back to Eugene which, as it happened, provided the nearest adequate landing field and a modest ceiling. After circling and coming down to ceiling level, the plane finished its descent in a literal deluge of rain. I was both relieved and grateful when the plane safely pulled up on the landing strip and did not at all mind dashing out through the downpour into the cosy waiting room with its crackling log fire.

After much telephoning, the Melchiors were located in the terminal manager's office at San Francisco. They agreed to go on to Portland by train for the concert there on the evening of the next day. The Eugene concert was canceled and played later on when, it so happened, there was one open date on the return trip from the Northwest.

The next day everyone finally got together with the Melchiors, the orchestra, and the chartered planes in Portland, and the tour was on after a rough start.

One of the first lessons to be learned in conducting road tours is not to divide members of a company in traveling from place to place. The manager thereby loses control of the situation, and no amount of alibis will make up for the confusion that could result. He has to be responsible for getting the personnel on time to fulfill the terms of each engagement. Deviation from this policy was forced in this case, for each plane carried one-half the personnel and luggage.

So much snow had drifted around the planes on the morning of our departure from Spokane that the motors of one of them could not be started without repairs. So I took off in the other plane with the Melchiors, the baggage, and part of the company for the next date in Vancouver; but first it was necessary to come down at Boeing Field in Seattle for customs and formalities. A message from the other plane said everything was OK and that it would follow only one-half hour later.

Coming into Vancouver by air presents a colorful spectacle on the grand scale. The approach is over a Chinese puzzle of interlocking segments of land and water—the pieces of landscape, bays, islands, woods, streams, clouds, and sky all perfectly fitted together into a stunning scenic panorama. Then as background, lush green forest-clad mountains stretch away from the city to the north. The pilot seemed not to have the slightest difficulty in steering his course through this scenic maze to the air terminal.

For hours nothing was either seen or heard of the second plane. Telephone and wire communication lines were so clogged that not until eight o'clock did word come through that the other plane had had an accident in landing at Seattle. As no one had authority to charter a special plane, valuable time was

99

lost in waiting, and it was not until ten o'clock that the formal concert program finally got under way at the university in Vancouver. In the meantime, Lauritz and those of the musicians on hand had kept the capacity house entertained. The concert finally concluded at midnight; then there was a party to attend, given by Danish friends.

The next morning there was still worse weather. In fact, there was no ceiling at all. The first plane had to be left behind, and, there being no special bus or rail facilities available, the Melchiors went ahead by private car while I waited at the bus terminal for the next regularly scheduled bus going to Seattle, into which company and luggage were finally piled.

There was scarcely a margin of an hour and a half between the time the company was due to arrive and curtain time. This was easily consumed by bad weather slowing up the run and more especially by provoking customs officials who must have noticed the company's state of mind and were, therefore, all the more deliberate about making their inspections. With my group I arrived at the Moore Theater in Seattle at 8:40 P.M., just as Lauritz was about to go on stage and calm any fears the audience might have as to the nonarrival of the remainder of his troupe.

Lauritz was a past master at performing this kind of emergency service, and there were three occasions on this tour when a matter of another two hours' delay would have meant no concerts. Lauritz Melchior invariably has his audience the moment he appears on the platform. Never flustered, he is completely at ease under any conditions. He merely has to smile, and the audience responds immediately with its complete confidence before a note is sung.

Like José Iturbi, however, he always had the unfortunate habit of figuring time too closely and not making allowance for contingencies. Even though the distance between hotel and concert hall may be short, anything can happen—a traffic tie-up, a flat tire, wrong directions, etc. It was early in 1938 that the Iturbis, José and Amparo, appeared for one of our engagements in a large city at just one minute before curtain time. And, in opening his spring tour down in Asheville two months later, Lauritz turned up just at curtain time. The company had left

New York two days earlier, but the Melchiors chose to take the last convenient plane out of New York. This plane was grounded en route, and the only rail connection barely made Asheville in time.

The third close call on this Pacific Coast tour is also worth recording, if only to show what tour planning behind a desk in New York can do to a manager on the road. Melchior and company played two nights in Seattle, after which both planes were on hand and ready for service again. After finishing all commitments north of San Francisco, the company laid off for a few days' rest; from then on it was a bus for the orchestra, and a plane or private car for the Melchiors.

While most of the jumps were reasonable, there was one terror. The company was booked into San Diego one night and into Sacramento on the following night—a distance of roughly 650 miles. And, according to the little green union books, a company was not supposed to travel more than three hundred miles per diem.

Rail transportation could not be worked out. So, immediately after the San Diego concert a special bus left, arriving in Hollywood, where most of the musicians lived, about 3:00 A.M. Five hours later they reassembled and, despite Sunday traffic, reached the auditorium in Sacramento about 8:00 P.M. There being no hotel space available, it must be explained that during that five-hour period I had planned to get at least four hours' sleep in the Melchiors' nearby Beverly Hills home. I picked up one of their cars from a nearby parking lot and loaded it with the music and such musical instruments as remained in the bus.

Known as the Viking, after Lauritz himself, their home was located on the Skyline Drive near the head of Laurel Canyon. To make matters as difficult as possible, the entire area was blanketed with one of those heavy, dripping fogs that make travel next to impossible. Anyway, I located the Skyline Drive but made the wrong turn and came out sometime later in Cahuenga Pass. From there back it was tortuous driving, with a steep slope on one side or the other. But they (the music scores, instruments, car, and driver) eventually arrived safely. The fog was so impenetrable that the break of dawn even passed unnoticed.

It was a considerable relief to have delivered the company in Sacramento and with almost no griping, but no one had either seen or heard from the Melchiors. They were to have reached Sacramento several hours before by plane direct from San Diego. With curtain time only minutes away, I dashed from a phone booth to literally bump into a breathless Kleinchen (Mrs. Melchior) in the foyer. To deepen the mystery, she was looking for Lauritz. In all the tours, anything or anybody could become separated sooner or later—but never the Melchiors. There were no messages or telegrams so one more call in desperation to the Hotel Senator confirmed that the sturdy Viking had just checked in.

Another ten minutes and the concert was on. Insofar as the audience was concerned, the few minutes' delayed opening was caused by getting the latecomers seated in a large capacity house. None of the performers, including the genial soloist, had eaten, but sandwiches and coffee were on hand at intermission, and the entire program was put over with gusto. Lauritz seemed to be more inspired than usual. Not only was he in excellent voice, but he made certain that the audience should come through with its participation in "Viva La Compagnie" as well. After singing the first verse solo, he always led the audience in succeeding verses. Usually, they responded in spirit, but in cities like San Francisco, White Plains, and Newark, only a Melchior could make them sing.

Kleinchen and Lauritz had had much more than their share of troubles that day. To begin with, the same thick fog with which I had become overly familiar at a very early hour had blanketed the whole of Southern California along the coast, grounding plane travel. So the Melchiors hired a private car and drove to Los Angeles, where the chauffeur got lost. They were an hour finding the airfield. Planes were flying again but off schedule, and crowds were waiting for cancellations on every flight. The resourceful Kleinchen, however, succeeded in getting a single cancellation for Lauritz on a plane going north.

Persistent Kleinchen was desperate. She was even ready to stowaway on the next flight when a Miss Griffith came to the rescue. She was to meet her mother that afternoon at

Sacramento but suddenly decided, instead, to meet her fiancé —
an army major — in Phoenix, Arizona. Kleinchen could have her
ticket if she would meet mother and explain, all of which
arrangements were duly consummated. The destination of
Lauritz's plane, however, turned out to be San Francisco, so the
changeover to a Sacramento plane accounted for his coming in
last.

As singer, artist, and showman, Melchior led a fabulous
career, aided and abetted by the inimitable Kleinchen. She
turned out to be truly "the girl I vas looking for" when, nearly
twenty-five years previously, this petite, vivacious, and very
charming little fraulein did actually descend via parachute,
right out of the blue, and land almost directly in the spacious
lap of the Heldentenor. At that time a total stranger, he was
busily slaking his thirst in a German beer garden. They were
not to remain strangers for long, however. They were scarcely
ever out of each other's sight subsequently.

Everything about the Lauritz and Maria (Kleinchen)
Melchior collaboration is just about as remarkable as their
introduction. Although she was self-effacing and satisfied to
remain in the background, his artistic career was built up step
by step largely as a result of her devoted efforts. She handled
her husband's engagements, helped in managing his business
affairs, supervised the household, and relieved him of a
multitude of details, troublesome and pleasant. "I make the
noise," he said once, "and she does everything else. She takes
away all the things that make a man restless and unhappy."
Otherwise, he could never have devoted himself so
wholeheartedly to his art — a most exacting taskmaster anytime.

Like Paul Robeson, Melchior was cast in a heroic mold. He
had, of course, been much more than a leading Metropolitan
singer in the grand tradition. As successor to the famous Jean de
Reszke, he more than doubled the late tenor's record in the
singing of Parsifal, Lohengrin, Siegmund, Tristan, Tannhäuser,
and Siegfried. According to the personally kept Melchior
statistics, he sang the latter role (6,534 words) 220 times. Then
he had an extensive concert repertoire to remember. Lauritz's
well-ordered meticulous mind also had other accomplishments.

He was, for instance, a complete master of gin rummy. He knew all the possible angles, for which he had devised a complicated method of perpetual scoring. I had acquired such a favorable impression of his affable disposition and even temper under the direst conditions of travel that it came as a slight shock to discover what can happen when mistakes are made at gin.

Above and beyond everything else, Lauritz was a master of the fine art of living. His hilltop home commanded the vast expanse of the San Fernando Valley, with its mountainous background on one side and overlooking Hollywood and other communities in its sweep down to the Pacific Ocean on the other side. As night descends, the whole region becomes converted into a veritable fairyland of twinkling lights, myriad colors ranged in a complication of designs all within one great pattern. It was here that the Melchiors and I returned by motor from the last concert of this hectic tour in the Pasadena Civic Auditorium, stopping en route for a midnight snack with Jean Hersholt and other Danish friends in Glendale.

Entering their house, they were quickly aware of a blaze of light and were greeted by Mutti, Kleinchen's mother. She had spent the evening decorating and lighting the Christmas tree to have it ready for their arrival. "Ooh, it's so beautiful," Kleinchen kept saying over and over. Lauritz was then inspired to an informal recital of the nostalgic carols, having already sung a concert and discoursed a couple of hours with friends. After more refreshments it was time for one of the familiar Havana cigars. (A shipment arrived annually from Cuba with the inscription, "From the best cigar maker in the world to the best tenor in the world.")

Having like children become very sentimental about Christmas, the Melchiors still were not through for the day, or, rather, for the night. On the table was a huge pile of unopened mail, providing the occasion for a renewed burst of activity. Like curious children they could not wait until everything was opened and read. With nothing more pressing about 6:00 A.M., they retired, though it is highly doubtful if, even then, their irrepressible energies had run down. The next afternoon Lauritz was off for a few days of duck hunting. Kleinchen was disposing of the mail with a secretary (between dozens of phone calls), and I was off for the airport.

14

The National Association of Concert Managers

*"The Presenter and the Producer
are the unfortunate prey
of the very elements that are
essential to their well-being."*
—Anonymous

It is a strange anomaly that the managers, presumably the brains of the presentations business, should have been so slow at taking steps to mutually solve their problems. As individuals they were almost powerless, but there were several reasons for this state of affairs.

In the first place, these rugged individualists are so individual that to arrive at a solution to some of their problems would be comparable only to getting agreement in the United Nations. True, there are always some problems peculiar to localities, but others of a more general character have persisted.

By the summer of 1948 there were at least three of the latter that had passed the aggravation stage and become threats to managerial well-being. This was enough to jar the managers into a meeting for the purpose of taking joint action. They were ready finally to admit that the time was ripe and that action was imperative. After feeling out the sentiment, I finally took the initiative and called a national meeting in New York City on December 14, 1948.

Concert managers from near and far who were on hand for this meeting are listed in the appendix. All these very worthy representatives of the "glamorous profession" were subsequently to be voted charter members of the new organization.

On the afternoon of the day previous, December 13, I met with Lulu Everts of Syracuse, Frank Andrews of Portland, Walter A. Fritschy of Atlanta, Arthur Oberfelder of Denver, and J. Herman Thuman of Cincinnati. All agreed thoroughly on the timeliness of a general meeting of local managers. Surprisingly enough, however, it was the encroachment of corporation-organized audiences into the territory of established, independent managers that dominated the discussion. The other immediate issues of ASCAP fees, admissions taxes, and exorbitant artists' fees also received a going-over; and it was agreed that these four problems would be placed ahead of other items on the agenda for the meeting.

The only other action taken was to invite Ward French, chairman of Columbia Artists Management, Inc., and O.O. Bottorff, president of National Concerts and Artists Corporation, to appear and state their respective policies to the assembled managers on the following day.

It was on the morning of December 14, 1948, that I called to order the meeting of managers who had assembled from all sections of the country at the Hotel Woodstock in New York City. I first read a telegram from the late Arthur See of Rochester, New York, which set the tone of the gathering: "Just returned from tour. . . . Sincerely hope managers will form real organization. Be assured of my interest and support. Would greatly appreciate knowing results. All best wishes."

Following the temporary chairman's comments on the need for forming an organization, Arthur Oberfelder of Denver was requested to take the chair pro tem, and he amplified and emphasized the former remarks. He stressed particularly the need for a solid front if managers were to survive and to master their formidable problems.

Elected as chairman of the meeting was Patrick Hayes of Washington, D.C. He was destined to serve as the energetic and personable president of the National Association of Concert

Managers for the next two years. Most of those present were seasoned managers who had been successfully operating in the profession through the golden days of concert giving. These were the times that the newly formed association would strive in vain to reactivate.

Elected as vice-president was Edna W. Saunders of Houston, Texas, foremost woman manager in the country and one of the grandest managers ever. J. Herman Thuman of Cincinnati, for forty-four years an outstanding and successful figure in the profession, was named treasurer. For eighteen years a concert manager in the metropolitan New York area, I became the first secretary, the duties of which I carried on for the next three years.

A directorate was selected, and committees were formed. But, of prime importance, for the first time in many years leading managers had come together and had a chance to face each other in open meeting and air their grievances. Everyone had so much on his mind to talk about that the opening session was carried over into the following day. After final adjournment, I was left with a pile of work—minutes to be written up, press stories to release, correspondence to issue, and a monthly bulletin to get out for members. So was begun the task of translating the work of the meeting into an active, going organization. Not the least of these tasks was the writing of a constitution and by-laws by a special committee, of which I was the chairman. Lawyer Samuel Blumenthal was of inestimable help in this department.

Probably one-half of the two-day meeting was devoted to hearing the four leading executives of the two dominant concert bureaus express their views. These were Marks Levine and O.O. Bottorff of National Concerts and Artists Corporation and Ward French and Fred C. Schang of Columbia Artists Management. The encroachment of their organized audiences on territory cultivated for so many years by some of the independent managers present was of special concern. They now saw their livelihoods being threatened by the very firms from which they were buying most of their talent.

The upshot of much talk and double-talk was that CAMI

finally agreed to sign up to stay out of cities within a radius of fifty miles if NCAC would agree to do likewise. The latter, however, stated that it might be agreeable but sidestepped the issue by declaring that such an agreement was probably illegal. There was so much quibbling at this time and subsequently that no agreement on this point was ever reached. More than likely the two bureaus had talked over their approach ahead of time. All that was ever accomplished was to put the brakes on their expansion efforts in certain areas.

A few years later, I was to have the opportunity in Kansas City to peruse the file of the late Arthur Wisner, the best organizer and salesman that Community Concerts Service ever had and its former president. In it were records of joint meetings held with Civic Concerts Service whereby cities and towns were traded like pawns, great care being taken not to give one company a population advantage over the other. It was these documents, showing evidence of collusion, that formed the basis subsequently for a suit by the Anti-Trust Division of the United States Department of Justice. As a result, these same two bureaus had to sign a consent decree limiting their monopolistic practices and making certain information, including their sponsors' lists, available to the managers generally as well as to the public.

The expansionist tendencies of the two agencies, however, were not basically curtailed. O.O. Bottorff later on boasted of having provided much of the language that went into the consent decree. Unquestionably, much of the strength of these bureaus, which controlled the bulk of concert artists and attractions, lay in their concert-giving departments—the community and civic concert appendages.

During a meeting at the time of which we are writing, Arthur Judson told us that only about one-half of their business was now attributable to independent concert managers. It was not only the organized audience movement, however, that was driving the legitimate managers into a corner where many were fighting for their existence; radio and television had taken their toll of live audiences as well.

Then, instead of less than fifty symphony orchestras around the country, there are now more than six hundred bidding for solo talent. They are all contributing to the vast lessening of the recital event in public favor and its probable extinction unless another era of giant solo talents should develop.

And, more important than any other factor, a shift in public taste was changing the inherent nature of the business. Why try to buck a trend? Dorothy and I were among the first of the innovators, and before long the novelties and ballets began to take precedence in subscription courses across the nation. Against the shrewd Schang's advice, it was in 1934 that we inserted Hurok's Ballet Russe de Monte Carlo in our recital series.

And, fifteen years later, we became the first management to include a dramatic event—*Don Juan in Hell*—among our subscription concert events. Zorah Berry of Buffalo was another farsighted concert manager who was prompt in doing the same, and others were to follow suit. Needless to say, the introduction of ballets and musical shows into concert courses was to prove of great assistance in bolstering the sagging returns from the strictly long-hair musical events. The fall of 1958 found *The Rivalry* (a dramatic show) included in thirty-eight major concert subscription series across the country.

In the first year of being, the National Association of Concert Managers was to complete its legal entity with a duly approved constitution and bylaws, add more members, inaugurate a helpful monthly bulletin to members, and achieve a settlement of the troublesome ASCAP fees matter whereby it was agreed that artists would split the royalty charges. There were, finally, hopeful signs in the offing that the admission taxes (enacted as a temporary wartime emergency levy) would at least be reduced from 20 percent to 10 percent.

No progress, however, was ever made toward the reduction of the even more exorbitant artists' fees. Sterling violinist though he was, Heifetz (among a few others) usually insisted on a $3,500 performance fee, although many was the time it was not earned at the box office. Managers could only console themselves with the prestige it added to the listing of his name among their season's events.

When it came to a showdown on this and some other vital issues, the board of the association failed to press its advantages.

There were always some managers afraid to incur the ill will of the two major bureaus and thus have their supply of talent choked off. On the other hand, the bureaus were apprehensive lest the association start in to acquire its own talent for its members on a wholesale basis. And the association should have become effective in negotiating with various unions to preclude their unilaterally taking actions that were both harmful and costly.

Unquestionably the association served some good purposes, especially in the exchanging of ideas and information. But its time came largely to be devoted to meetings, and then more meetings, where all had a chance to compare notes, air their grievances, and listen to speeches. Socializing also became an important activity — attending cocktail parties, dinners, and the theater.

I was never in favor of limiting membership strictly to managers of concerts; I wanted the membership to be all-embracing, including lecture and town hall series, theater managements, and all important classifications of the presentations business.

In passing, occasion must be taken to pay tribute to the late Charles A. Sink, second president of the National Association of Concert Managers. At that time dean of American concert managers, he brought prestige and distinction to the organization by reason of his efforts on its behalf. Possessed of great personal charm and an able executive, he was for nearly fifty years the director of the famed Ann Arbor Music Festival.

The association continued to augment its membership from year to year. Its increasing strength was negated eleven years later, however, when a large segment of the college and university directors of cultural events broke away and formed its own association. The possibility of realizing the ideal of a strong, all-embracing association of local managers, or presenters, appears to be still in the future.

The new group, known as the Association of College, University, and Community Arts Administrators, has blossomed and grown to twice the size of the parent organization. Total membership in all is now twenty times that of the original group, the name of which has been changed to International Society of Performing Arts Administrators.

15

*Artists and *Audiences

*"It is obvious that, with all
the improvement in
radio transmission and
reception, it is not and
never can be, as satisfying
as the actual performance
of music by living
artists in the flesh."*
—John Tasker Howard

In all audiences, whether of a concert or of a play, there are all kinds of people who have come for many different reasons. Most of them have the ability in common to surrender to the beauty of an experience and to the comfort and congeniality of their surroundings. It is said that an audience, or any crowd of people, differs as a group from any and all component parts. This is what makes for excitement in bringing artists and audiences together—one cannot always be certain of the event's outcome.

The psychologists contend that a crowd is not a mere aggregation of people; it is a state of mind. And, a century ago, in Goethe's prologue to *Faust*, the manager talks to the poet about the audience at the play.

> Think, too, for whom you write, I pray
> One comes to while an hour away;
> One from the festive board, a sated guest

Others, more dreaded than the rest
From journal reading hurry to the play,
As to a masquerade, with absent minds they press
Sheer curiosity their footsteps winging.
Ladies display their persons and their dress,
Actors unpaid, their service bringing.
What puts a full house in a merry mood?
More closely view your partners of the night
The half are cold, the half are rude.

It is the wise manager who realizes that all these people are among his audience, in addition to those who have come because they are true music lovers or ardent playgoers, as the case may be.

There is another element that joins the dissimilar tastes of concert or playgoers. Very few tickets are sold singly, for a pleasure shared is a pleasure doubled. Many a wife who enjoys every note of a concert has persuaded her husband and family to go with her in the hope that they, too, may derive pleasure from it.

The advance preparation on the part of the sponsor or management includes the preparation of his public for the event they are to experience. Knowledge of the background of the concert artist, the kind of person he is, and especially the numbers to be included in the program itself make for an audience that is expectant. A mood of excitement can be created in advance. Lack of attention to the routine duties of the staff and facilities of the auditorium or theater itself can spoil an otherwise perfect evening.

Usually the first actual contact of the public with the event is through the box office. Efficient, pleasant ticket sellers can do much toward a warm customer relationship. The unreasonable customer is in the minority but invariably exaggerates his importance by the noise he makes. During the night of an event a clever box-office treasurer soon learns to spot the customer on line who demands the seats reserved for her, though she (or he) knows the reservation had never been made and the tickets probably would not have been held until the night of the event in any case.

Westchester County Center box-office personnel kept customers good-naturedly in hand for all the years of our presentations and still managed to retain a sense of humor. They claimed that the main requirements for a good box-office treasurer are first to be a mind reader; to look pleasant but not surprised when asked for a balcony seat downstairs or for two "standing room" together; to have at hand the latest weather report, timetables, and information—all so you will know the answer to any question. And, above all, concede that the customer is always right.

Tact is required to handle the customer who sends in a large check for tickets with the request to return it if she cannot receive tickets for the eighth row center. There must always be a few perfect seats up one's sleeves to cover errors and those unavoidable requests when the governor or some other notable makes a last-minute decision to attend. There is no rule governing seat preferences, except that for a piano concert all seats should be on the left side of the house! There has been serious discussion about having a mirror to reflect the pianist's hands so that those on the right side of the hall could see the keyboard as well.

The box office must find choice seat locations for those friends of the manager (whom he does not remember) on the night of a sellout and take care of extra press requests on a capacity night. Invariably on a night of "Standing Room Only," a representative of one of the New York papers would show up with a pass, although he was not reviewing the concert and only some dire calamity would have produced a story. Heavy press requests in advance are usually a good omen, for they smell out success.

Many unusual friends have resulted from subscriber contacts, some of whom retained their same seats for twenty years. In that twentieth year, on a motor trip in the West, we were greeted on the top of Loveland Pass near Denver by one of these subscribers, Mrs. Jack Naylor, who got out of the car parked by sheer chance next to ours and thanked us for her years of pleasure in attending our concerts. In fact, we have met former subscribers in such remote places as Yellowstone Park; Amarillo, Texas; on a Broadway bus; in mid-Atlantic on the

Queen Mary; once on a cruise in the Caribbean; and in other out-of-the-way places.

Not so grateful was the subscriber whose seats had been next to a post in the last row of the balcony. As soon as there was an opportunity, she was moved closer to the stage, which brought an irate phone call asking for the same seats back; it seemed that her mother liked to lean against the adjoining post whenever she fell asleep.

One of the real intangibles of the relationship between artist and audience is the acoustics. If one cannot hear without effort, then all the brilliance of the talent is of no avail. Some halls get a reputation for perfect acoustics and some for bad acoustics, which may actually apply to only a few restricted seat locations. A spot just beneath the highest point of a dome is sometimes dead, but the public discusses the complicated subject of acoustics with as much familiarity as if it were a new car or the weather, and with as many differences of opinion.

It is not enough to have ushers trained to seat an audience correctly and quickly; they must also understand that part of the job is to be alert throughout the evening and to help in solving any problem that may arise. Even after the program has started, the good manager does not relax, for he has to check the temperature and the sound; check out the box-office statement; and watch the show so that he will know whether the audience reaction is good or bad and whether the critic is fair or unfair. Latecomers must be made satisfied to stand in the back through the first part of the program, and the right seat location must be found for the customer who has lost his tickets. He must be ready to have the lighting changed when the artist storms into the wings and says it is too bright; and then he must calm the concertgoer who is unable to see to read the program notes.

Perhaps a careless sponsor, interested only in ticket sales, caused the remark in a letter received from Tyrone Power while on tour with *John Brown's Body*. "The show improves daily," he wrote, "and if only the auditoriums did too, we would be completely happy." We have even known an artist's name to be misspelled on the marquee—that manager never knew how near he was to having no show when the artist discovered the error.

Isaac Stern, noted violinist, had sound views on program making which were widely quoted when he was only twenty-six years of age. "Simple—just play what you like. If you play a piece because it's the right length, or you need something light, or something showy, just here in the program, or because other people like it—I mean, if you don't like it yourself, you aren't going to make your audience like it. What you are playing at any given moment is your favorite. We are playing it because it has meaning for you and you want to communicate its meaning to your audience." There are several facets of music to be included—the classics and the moderns as well as the war-horses, or the works that are supposed to be most popular among the classics at the moment.

A woman artist can add to the enjoyment of a concert by her appearance. Lily Pons and Ethel Bartlett were both outspoken in their belief that concertgoers are clothes conscious. The right type gown to complement her personality is all important; then it must harmonize with the background. All colors designed for stage use must be chosen under brilliant artificial light, which has a devastating effect on some normally beautiful and striking colors. Miss Bartlett favored brilliant, primary colors—using gold, silver, red, and yellow. She had her secretary write ahead to know the color of the stage background; and then she brought several gowns, which were tried on stage a few hours before the concert. The result was a gold brocade against a soft blue background with great bowls of forsythia on each side of the stage. The whole ensemble made a stunning appearance and got a pleasant audience reaction before she had played a note.

There is a condition over which the artist has little control, and which sometimes governs his mood on arrival. Touring requires many hours of travel in all kinds of weather and conveyances. There are bound to be tight schedules; Rachmaninoff once said that his life was one long tour, and Heifetz once wrote his own epitaph as follows:

> Killed in action by a Flying Staccato
> So here are lying his remains
> No more concerts, no more trains.

In a merrier vein, Fred Schang of Columbia Concerts once sent a holiday greeting that included quips from some of the artists under his management:

> Said Nelson Eddy to Charlie Kullman:
> "Most of our lives we spent in a Pullman."
> "Okay by me if the pay is steady,"
> Said Charlie Kullman to Nelson Eddy.

Most artists like to arrive in plenty of time, which is a source of comfort to the nerves of the management. On one icy, wintry evening, an early comer came to the box office and said, "Hello, here is your artist." Such was the modesty of Josef Hofmann, who had come on an early train with his wife, then had a bite at the lunch wagon across the street because he did not wish to disturb anyone.

Everything possible should be done to start a stage performance on time and without confusion. Artists are keyed up to the announced curtain time and, hence, nervous at the outset—not from inexperience, but as Rubinstein explains it, "We know we have to do our best at 8:30. It is not like a composer who can say, 'Well, I don't feel like composing today, I'll go out to the beach for the day.'"

There is something exciting about the power that many important artists possess to come on the stage and, by just standing still, quiet an audience of thousands. Soon we know whether that collaboration between artist and audience, that sort of interaction, is taking place. It does not always happen, for they may not be sympathetic to each other, but when it does, both the artist and the audience enjoy a rapport that is conducive to an inspired performance.

A wildly enthusiastic audience gets tremendous results from the performer. Sometimes applause comes too soon or in the wrong place. After a Philadelphia Orchestra concert, Eugene Ormandy once came off the stage remarking to us, "That audience knows when to applaud." During intermission, the management is usually trying to check the reactions to the performance. One is reminded of Paul Whiteman's comment, "If this concert has any message at all, let it be this: enjoy it or be bored by it, but stop worrying about its message."

There are sometimes unexpected and trying moments when the experience of the performer comes to his aid. Such was the case when José Iturbi was conducting the Rochester Symphony Orchestra and his young son-in-law, Stephen Hero, was playing the violin for the first time under his noted father-in-law's baton. A string broke near the opening of Mendelssohn's Concerto in E Minor. Iturbi stopped the orchestra, turned to the audience with a smile, and said, "Please excuse." Thus neither he nor the audience was embarrassed, and they began the concerto over again after the string had been replaced.

Before the last curtain, arrangements should have been made for the stage doors to be guarded and the artist protected from distant relatives (who appear in every town); souvenir seekers, who will sometimes take the buttons off his coat if possible; too great a number of autograph hounds; too eager photographers, unsolicited interviews; and cranks! At the same time the artist must be given the opportunity to get his breath and prepare to greet the long lines of sincere people who have made up the audience and wish to show their gratitude and to take away in their memories a close-up of the celebrity.

Many times when the members of the audience had shown pleasure at the experience shared, there came to mind the beautiful statement made by Lotte Lehmann during World War II: "I make music. Music is my world, a world far lovelier, more immaculate and more blessed than all the politics on earth. Music brings nations together, politics divides them. Music is God's gift, politics is man's work."

We are reminded of the girl in Thornton Wilder's *Our Town* who in heaven wishes to relive one beautiful day or hour, and upon returning to earth, she realizes that the simplest day or hour was filled with much beauty which she had not understood while living it.

Dr. Walter Damrosch inscribed this picture: "For Julian Olney. To my friend and fellow worker with best wishes for the music of the World's Fair of 1939."

Gen. James G. Harbord, Mrs. Julian Olney, and Rt. Hon. Winston Churchill at reception in the statesman's honor on March 8, 1932.

Lily Pons and Mrs. Olney meet in 1934 to plan one of the French diva's first concerts in America.

Lily Pons, "queen of the coloratura range," preparing for a concert.

Martin Johnson, noted African explorer, and pygmy friends.

José Iturbi, popular Spanish pianist.

Yehudi Menuhin, one of the violin greats of all time.

Fritz Kreisler, world famous violinist through two generations.

Sergei Rachmaninoff, legendary Russian pianist and composer, was a favorite repeat performer.

Josef Hofmann, superb American pianist.

Lucretia Bori, lovely Spanish star of opera and concert.

Marian Anderson, one of America's most beloved singers.

Alexandra Danilova and Léonide Massine in *Gaité Parisienne*.

Mia Slavenska, a star of the Ballet Russe de Monte Carlo.

Ethel Barrymore, queen of America's royal family of the theatre.

Tallulah Bankhead starring in *The Second Mrs. Tanqueray* at the Ridgeway Theatre.

Gracie Fields, once the most popular music hall performer in England, never failed to entertain with her inimitable songs and handsprings.

Eugene Ormandy, the renowned conductor of the Philadelphia Orchestra from 1936 to 1979.

Leopold Stokowski, flamboyant conductor of the Philadelphia Orchestra from 1914 to 1936.

Tyrone Power, Anne Baxter, and Raymond Massey in *John Brown's Body*.

Harry Belafonte, Marge and Gower Champion in the musical revue *Three for Tonight*.

The brilliant Norwegian opera and concert soprano Kirsten Flagstad (center), daughter Elsa, and Mrs. Olney.

Originating their unique shows in Hollywood, the Laughton-Gregory firm had the casts of two shows rehearsing simultaneously in the same building. Standing: Lloyd Nolan, Tyrone Power, Raymond Massey and John Hodiak. Seated: Charles Laughton, Anne Baxter, Dick Powell and Henry Fonda.

Vladimir Horowitz, piano perfectionist.

Artur Rubinstein, pianist extraordinary.

Harold McGee (director), Paul Robeson, and Mrs. Olney appear delighted over plans for staging O'Neill's *The Emperor Jones*.

Gary Merrill, Bette Davis, Carl Sandburg, and Norman Corwin in a happy mood over their forthcoming show.

Mrs. Olney entering gateway of the ancient Roman wall at Pevensey in England during filming of *Great Castles of Britain*.

Directors attending board meeting of the National Association of Concert Managers in 1953 at Gatlinburg, Tennessee, (standing left to right) Charles A. Sink, Roland E. Chesley, Mrs. Frost, William K. Huff, Ralph W. Frost, Mrs. Huff, Julius Bloom, Marvin McDonald, and A. E. Grove. Seated are Mrs. Sink, Zorah B. Berry, Edna W. Saunders, Lillian P. Bonney, and Mrs. Olney.

The First Drama Quartette made theatrical history in Bernard Shaw's *Don Juan in Hell*. Charles Laughton, Charles Boyer, Agnes Moorehead, Sir Cedric Hardwicke.

Lauritz Melchior, the most magnetic singing actor since Chaliapin, the eminent Danish Heldentenor was an audience favorite in opera, concert and the movies.

Sigmund Romberg, popular composer of 72 operettas and musicals, formed and conducted his own orchestra on national tour in 1942.

Leonard Bernstein as he appeared in 1947 when conducting the Boston Symphony Orchestra for the Olney Concert Series; and as he is today at the height of his achievements.

Part Two

The Next Twenty Years

NO NEED FOR PROGRAM NOTES

There is no need for program notes for those
Who hear concertos in a gurgling brook
And never doubt the virtuosity
Of wind in lyric exercise. No look
Of inquiry is wanted to confirm
The overtones produced by aspen leaves
Or osier twigs upon a bank.
The thrush, whose deep-throat ecstasy tone-weaves
A fabric rich in subtle harmonies,
Encauls within the grottoes of men's hearts
Sweet memories of stirring sonic hues,
Enshrining melodies never meant for charts.

—Julius Grodenchik in the
Christian Science Monitor

16

Beginnings of an Association

*"It must not be forgotten
that the arts are an
important part of
civilization."*
*—from notice posted in
Opera House, Moscow*

Sometime in the early fall of 1948, my office telephone in White Plains rang, and a confident, compelling voice said, "Hello, this is Paul Gregory. I'm manager of the concert department for Music Corporation of America, and I want to talk to you about our shows." Thus began an acquaintanceship that was soon to ripen into a close association.

Incidentally, this was also the first manifestation of a many-faceted personality. As new aspects came into play, it was to trace a new road to achievement in the theater. The effect could well leave a lasting impression in the methods and style of those who create the make-believe world behind the proscenium arch. Call them impresarios, producers, or whatever else; it is they who provide the spark that makes for a memorable evening in the theater.

More often than not, however, the original flash dissipates itself. What happened in Gregory's case invites study, especially because the original promise did sustain itself throughout

139

several successes. Beyond an extraordinary talent for salesmanship, he had other important assets. These included creative ability, artistic sensitiveness, tremendous vitality, and unlimited ambition.

In Gregory's case, with the addition of luck (he once estimated it at 50 percent), these various ingredients produced in succession four smash stage successes, three major successes on TV, and a good motion picture. Here all at once was achievement in three mediums—all in the brief space of five years. And he was still only in his mid-thirties.

The scarcest but most important single talent in the field of entertainment is the creative manager or producer. An independent spirit seeking self-realization for a dreary decade before success arrived, Paul found the going rough, though rewarding. Slow to take advice, he had to rely principally on his own ingenuity and resources in the beginning—at least until Charles Laughton entered the scene.

The immediate result of that momentous phone call was that our office found itself saddled with thirty thousand dollars worth of commitments for attractions that they had never expected to sponsor. Spike Jones and his City Slickers, Horace Heidt (cashing in on amateur talent), and other attractions temporarily benefited by their sponsorship.

Then one day Paul returned from a trip to Hollywood and his first encounter with Charles Laughton. The famed actor was then hardly more than a name on the long MCA roster of talent and almost inactive. I recall only too well impatiently listening to an extended recital all about this great talent and theater personality and what could be done with him. A packet of intriguing snapshots was produced, showing Laughton in a variety of poses, surrounded by the books in his library.

The enthusiasm was contagious, indeed, and I could not wait to hear the new reading program (having long been an admirer of Laughton, the actor), but I commented that selling the performances around the country would be more than just difficult. MCA did not think he could be sold at all in such programs. Reading the Bible, especially, could scarcely be considered commercial. So Paul had to prove the impossible almost single-handedly. And thus began one of the memorable collaborations of present-day theater.

On weekends spent at our hilltop home in Westchester, Paul gave increasing evidence of dissatisfaction with the limitations of his MCA job. Ever restless, he had now glimpsed, through Charles Laughton, a theater world of which he had always dreamed as far back as he could remember. Possessed of a powerful imagination and having tasted the first fruits of achievement—the press reviews were superb—Paul saw this first Laughton tour as the touchstone of more successes to come. He began talking about going into business for himself.

Some months passed. Then word came one day from Hollywood that Paul now had his own agency, with Charles Laughton as the first client. In fact, they had gone into business together and shared the ownership of the new firm, Gregory Associates, Inc. They had new production ideas which they were anxious to realize.

Having been out of pictures for nearly three years, Laughton, it seemed to many, had had his career. Who could forget his memorable characterizations in *Ruggles of Red Gap*, *Quartet*, *Mutiny on the Bounty*, *Hobson's Choice*, *King Henry VIII*, and others?

But Laughton had dreams too; there were still other worlds to conquer. In the meantime, the first reading tour was followed by a second, then a third, and still more. The programs were skillfully selected and put together from the gleanings of much reading and research. Effortless though they appeared from a seat in the audience, they were arranged with consummate art and were deftly staged. Other artists attempted to emulate this odd species of success, but to no avail. Next, Laughton made a TV series. Then came picture offers again.

In fact, from coast to coast came demands for engagements. Backed by the Gregory salesmanship, his picture fee was boosted to an all-time high for a part he detested—King Herod in *Salome*. All this, however, was by way of transition; Charles Laughton wanted to become a director.

After several abortive attempts, he was ready now for the new assignment. The story of resulting triumphs will be told sub-

141

sequently; but here a word about the method. Stagecraft is an art best learned by the practice. The ideal basis from which to start is the establishment of a genuine rapport between producer and director (with the assistance of a bank roll). The Charles Laughton–Paul Gregory business partnership also became an artistic collaboration.

As a sidelight on Charles Laughton's artistic proclivities, his ability to develop acting talent and his mastery of stagecraft are only too well known. He was also a shrewd and knowing art collector. He had examples of the works of Pierre Auguste Renoir, Georges Seurat, and other French impressionists; he collected drawings of Morris Graves long before that artist became famous; his catholic taste went to Japanese art as well as to that of other countries, not to overlook the Mexican Siquieros. Then there was his large collection of pre-Columbian artifacts, which were sold at the Parke-Bernet Galleries after his passing.

The piéce de resistance was one of the celebrated Renoirs titled *The Bathers*. This huge canvas hung at the foot of Laughton's bed until finally purchased by an anonymous art patron for the Metropolitan Museum of Art. Laughton had his collaborator, Professor Bush, brought into his home to lie in his own bed so that Bush could spend the last days of his fatal illness gazing on *The Bathers*.

Every spring Charles Laughton never failed to hire a limousine so that he could be driven through the hills ringing the lower end of the San Joaquin Valley and gaze on the vast fields of the wild flowers at the height of their bloom, always a noted tourist attraction.

Speaking of flowers—Laughton had a penchant for the night-blooming cereus, of which he had several potted examples at the side of his swimming pool. Dorothy and I had been alerted well ahead to expect a call some night—that we must immediately drop everything and go over to view these exotic plants on the one night of the year when they chose to burst into bloom.

After much anticipation, we finally got the telephone call. It was nearly midnight when we arrived. The gorgeous blooms were well worth the trip. But that was not all; there was a bonus attraction. The pool itself was populated by a number of

Hollywood notables (male and female) paddling about in the only attire provided by nature.

Charles Laughton could also be thoughtful on occasion. When we departed for Europe in the spring of 1954 to make the grand tour for the first time, he arranged for his innkeeper brother Tom to host us at his Royal Inn in Scarborough. Here we were accommodated in the Prince of Wales Suite overlooking the North Sea.

Tom Laughton also provided a car driven by the same chauffeur who had occasionally driven brother Charles through the enchanting countryside. Places visited included the stark moors made famous by the Brontës (whose graves we visited), the stark ruins of Whitby and Rivaulx abbeys and Scarborough Castle, and other fascinating locales.

It was on Laughton's insistence that we drove up the beautiful Moselle Valley from Coblenz in West Germany. At historic Kochem we bought two cases of choice Rosenberg wine, which was shipped to our home in California. There it was refused entry by U.S. Customs. Two years later I bought them back at a public sale of confiscated items.

Charles Laughton lived with each directorial assignment from the beginning. Where it was an original piece, he labored side by side with the author or adapter to make it structurally sound. By the time it went into production, he probably knew every word of the script backwards. Like the artist rendering his oil paintings, his was the master hand that finally achieved an artistic entity.

The wedding of this talent with Gregory's pragmatism and flair for showmanship was not all sweetness and light. Although their respective gifts complemented each other in a remarkable manner, battles royal were carried on through many a weekend, but with constructive results. And, what is even more interesting, they became commercially sound and paid off. But, then, should not the best art bring the best returns?

The introduction of Dorothy and me into the Gregory Associates operation came in 1952, thus completing a well-rounded producing complex. For six years there was to be associated in one company in one office all the essential elements of a completely integrated production firm. Experienced managerial and booking abilities were brought in by producer Gregory to complement, as well as implement, Laughton's artistic achievements.

Neither Laughton nor Gregory ever fully appreciated the significance and potential of such a welding of talents, or they would have been more tolerant of each other and more conscious of the ultimate potential. During the period of this triple association it was possible to start with a bare idea and then see it through the various production stages to its ultimate market. It was my job to develop and exploit this market. My booking office was separate but near enough to maintain liaison with the production activities.

Dorothy Olney's role in the operation was to take some of the load off Gregory and "follow through." She organized and ran his office, made up the budgets, kept statistics, set up an accounting procedure, and acted as consultant at any hour of the day or night. Not a small part of the job was the constant encouragement necessary, for Paul had a tendency to tire of an idea once it had been launched. Also, his impatience and intolerance led him into many personal conflicts that had to be ironed out.

Such a complete operation is rare, so, once established, it should never have been allowed to lapse and disintegrate. Gregory, however, was not one to delegate authority. While it lasted, the collaboration represented a unique innovation in theater technique—a contribution that was to make theater history.

17

Don Juan in Hell

> "Have you walked up and
> down the earth lately? I have,
> and I have examined Man's
> wonderful inventions. And
> I tell you that in the arts of
> life man invents nothing;
> but in the arts of death he
> outdoes Nature herself."
> —Bernard Shaw

It was to be expected that Charles Laughton would not be satisfied too long with the one-man programs. He was an avid reader with an extensive knowledge of dramatic literature. From time to time he tried experiments in offbeat productions. Now another idea emerged: a stage presentation of the long-neglected Don Juan sequence from Bernard Shaw's *Man And Superman*.

Paul Gregory's vivid imagination was not slow in seeing the potentials. He promptly proceeded to get the rights while Laughton enlisted the interest of Charles Boyer and Sir Cedric Hardwicke, both old friends. The fourth member to be added to an already distinguished cast was Agnes Moorehead.

About two-thirty on a Westchester midwinter morning in 1951, a call came from the Hollywood operator—Paul Gregory was on the line. Would I, he asked, put on his *Don Juan in Hell* in Washington, D.C., sometime in the early spring? I was not slow in agreeing to do so, having been waiting weeks for word of

145

this impending attraction. No contracts, however, were sent on, so nothing was done beyond setting a tentative date for March 8 in Constitution Hall.

Two weeks passed. Then another call came from the same source. How was the Washington date progressing? the harried Gregory voice inquired. I quickly replied that everything was in the works and that I would get back with a report of ticket sales in short order. It was useless to mention a contract at this point, but what about the terms of the engagement? Oh, well, I thought, best not to make mention of these either, but no time could be lost at this point.

With three weeks remaining before March 8, 1951, I got on the next plane to Washington. Tickets were ordered, to be placed on sale immediately; dramatic editors of the four leading newspapers were called on in the interest of the press campaign; and an advertising schedule was ordered. Results: second-highest gross receipts of the new touring *Don Juan in Hell* and press notices that left nothing to be desired.

It was at the time of this performance that I first made the acquaintance of Charles Laughton at luncheon and was told the story of the inception of this unique attraction. It seems that Charles, in his own words, had "slept with the book under my pillow for twenty-five years" and had dreamed of someday bringing this piece to life in some manner on stage. As originally written by Bernard Shaw, *Man and Superman* was four hours in length. The "Hell" scene, however, was ordinarily omitted. Long and apparently tedious, it had never been successfully played. And, in any event, the drama was the usual show length without this sequence. So, for fifty years, here was an original G.B.S. script waiting for an inspired production.

And, as Shaw one day admitted, this particular scene was not intended to be played in any case. "However, young man," said the elderly playwright to Paul over the trans-Atlantic telephone when he persisted in going ahead, "I cannot honestly advise you to experiment with it; but I should certainly like you to try it." He even made attractive terms—unheard of in the long history of canny Shaw negotiations. Unfortunately, Shaw never saw the Laughton–Gregory production, for he passed away before the company reached England in the summer of that year. Shortly before his death, Shaw had warned that Don Juan was a "fountain of words." Laughton wrote back, "Yes—but what words."

Setting up the initial production of *Don Juan in Hell* was anything but easy. The piece requires the services of four mature, personable acting talents of star caliber who can work in harmony. There is no action on stage—they merely talk—and Charles Laughton's staging was simplicity itself. All in evening dress, the four stars, billed as "The First Drama Quartette," sat on or stood before high black stools in front of which were reading stands, each supporting a huge bound script. Although the actors presumably were reading from these books, they served chiefly as props, inasmuch as each one knew his respective lines.

With the actors on two-week contracts only, the first engagements got off to a wobbly start. An initial break-in performance was given in a small hall at Claremont College. Then, as the performance gained in its impact and acquired momentum, more engagements were booked, resulting finally in a coast-to-coast tour. As an initial effort to secure these bookings, a list of one hundred top sponsors was made up. Then a carefully drafted sales letter was directed to them, announcing the attraction. These brought in all of six responses, including one offer of a booking at a fee of $1,000— anything but an auspicious beginning.

Charles Laughton as the Devil, Charles Boyer as Don Juan, Agnes Moorehead as Dona Anna, and Sir Cedric Hardwicke as the Statue all turned in stellar performances. Reviews from coast to coast were raves from the outset. As one typical press comment stated the situation, "By simply standing on a stage for two hours and debating the relative merits of Heaven and Hell and of man's life-force versus his death-love, four actors have been packing theaters across the United States."

Having triumphantly played its way from the West Coast, the company made its first important eastern appearance in the huge Constitution Hall in Washington, D.C. Wrote the *Washington Post*, "After sensational successes in the West, the

147

latest 'freak' of the entertainment world arrived in the East last night and conquered an audience of 3700 at Constitution Hall . . . , four persons on a sceneryless stage reciting a one-act play written fifty years ago hardly suggests an evening of wit . . . . The result is a fascinating, provocative evening."

On the following September 23, touring was resumed in Amarillo, Texas, and tickets were bought as eagerly by the ranchers of the prairie country as they had been during the first tour by the intelligentsia in the big cities. Now, the attraction was finally headed for Broadway. The performance, however, had not been thought of in terms of a theater piece to run for a period in the usual legit playhouse. Instead, it was cautiously booked into Carnegie Hall for the evening of October 22, 1951. As the drama writer on one of the New York dailies phrased it "New York is to be just another one-night stand on the tour this season of the First Drama Quartette." In any event, the ticket sale was announced on a Sunday, three weeks ahead, and by noon of the following day there were no unsold tickets.

In the meantime, the word was getting around, and the momentum on tour was picking up. The producer's share in one city (three performances) jumped to $12,124; another city turned over $5,943 as the company's share of a single engagement; and in a third city producer Gregory garnered $17,367 for himself. By the time the fateful October 22 had arrived, indications clearly pointed to a Broadway theater. The reviews on Tuesday morning made it imperative. Paul had no inclination to wait up and face these notices, but at 5:00 A.M. Dorothy had all the morning dailies, had located the respective ecstatic notices, then awakened Paul, and read them all word for word over the telephone. The following samplings were typical of the attitude of the Metropolitan press on this extraordinary event.

Long Lost Art Revived by Four Actors Here. Drama Quartet in *Don Juan in Hell* Goes in for Unabashed Acting. Four actors play tennis with Shaw's mettlesome dialogue. It is one of those theatrical ironies that the most stimulating show in New York last night is no longer available this morning.
— Walter Kerr, New York *Herald Tribune*

Like everything good in this world, it has to be seen to be believed: and now Gothamites and Brooklynites can join the rest of the country in regarding it as a masterpiece.

This is a performance compounded of sheer skill, and it will never be forgotten by anyone in Carnegie Hall last evening.

— Brooks Atkinson, *New York Times*

Decades from now those of us who are around will find occasion still to talk about the First Drama Quartette . . . . The show is a mental limbering exercise, a relaxing pasttime, or a gay appeal to the imagination. Call it a radiantly dramatized lecture, or a play designed to ardently inspire your own invention. Either way it is unforgettable.

If it had previously seemed a stunt, Manhattan by its own peculiar tough test, gave it the final approbation. From now on it can only be freakish in the voracious demand for tickets.

— William Hawkins, New York *World Telegram & Sun*

Four charming actors present one of Shaw's richest talkfests.

— John Chapman, New York *Daily News*

Nothing Broadway has had to offer of recent years has been more absorbing than this theatrically unorthodox presentation of a play which is not a play in the ordinary sense.

— John Mason Brown, *Saturday Review*

At least one incident of the Carnegie Hall engagement should be noted in passing. It was discovered too late that the usual tickets reserved for the opening night press were all in the wrong locations. It was now decided that the usual press list was a "must" and had to be accommodated if the show was to run subsequently in a Broadway theater. The arduous task of retrieving tickets already sold for the favored seat locations of the critical fraternity and substituting therefor tickets for inferior locations was assigned to the tactful Dorothy, the ticket wizard. She managed the entire exchange successfully, except for one holdout — a theatrical manager who would have been expected to appreciate her unhappy situation and, therefore, cooperate.

In commenting on the circumstances for the *New York Times* in a special article, Arthur Gelb wrote,

> Hastily consulting its list of mail-order ticket holders who were in possession of a portion of the hall's 2,760 seats, the management dispatched telegrams and emissaries to those who had the choicest reservations, stating its embarrassment at the fix in which it found itself and pleading for the return of the tickets.
>
> The response to these unorthodox tactics was mixed. Some refused point-blank; others were persuaded to exchange their reservations for later performances in Westchester, Connecticut, or New Jersey. One woman agreed to swap her tickets for an almost equally scarce pair to the White Plains presentation of the Sadler's Wells Ballet in March; a second woman, before she would capitulate, had to be promised a backstage introduction to Charles Boyer, a member of the cast; another, told that her third row aisle locations were being solicited for one of the critics, said she would exchange them for inferior seats in Carnegie Hall, provided they would afford her a view of his head.

Immediately following this metropolitan debut of the first Gregory attraction, we played in succession White Plains, Greenwich, Newark, and Hartford. There was a sixth appearance at the Brooklyn Academy of Music. Then there was a hole in the subsequent itinerary on November 16 and 17, which the route dictated should be logically played in Rochester, New York; and Columbus, Ohio. Timid local managements, however, balked at the fee (now up to $3,000), so I took these contracts. Even I was surprised at the gross receipts on the two performances, which aggregated $19,505.

Road engagements had been contracted to the end of November, but arrangements were soon made to go into a Broadway theater immediately thereafter. There was another Sunday announcement, and another avalanche of mail orders. This time, however, it was ten times greater than before, the immediate flood of mail orders bringing into the box office close to $100,000.

The limited number of legitimate playhouses available (about one-third of the prewar supply) made only a five-week engagement at the Century Theater possible. Cautious press agent Karl Bernstein advised that one never opens a show in New York, closes, then reopens, and expects the public to respond. But this was "something new in the theater," and the company returned in the early spring of 1952 for a third engagement in the same season. At the Plymouth Theater the now-famous troupe was to perform for another eight weeks.

The "show must go on" theory enables many a producer to face tense situations without hesitation because he has no choice. At the Century Theater in New York City, *Don Juan* played on Sunday nights so that the cast could see shows on Monday nights. Imagine, if you can, at 8:00 P.M. on a Sunday, Mr. Laughton breaking one of his dentures just as he was leaving for the theater. Imagine also not only *finding* a dentist in a three-block radius but finding one willing to immediately make repairs so that Mr. Laughton could perform. I rushed to the theater and made an announcement that the performance would be delayed; Dorothy rushed to the dentist with Charles; the dentist hurriedly installed something temporary; then, with his coattails flying as he ran, and looking like the Shaw devil he was about to impersonate, Mr. Laughton arrived on stage breathless but intact at 9:15 P.M.

Up to this point, road engagements had been booked almost single-handedly by Paul Gregory, with the assistance of a booker in the Middle West and another in the East. Plans were soon in the making for the season of 1952–1953. It was decided to continue *Don Juan in Hell* for a third trek around the country. I was asked to become eastern representative and arrange the playing time.

Don Juan in Hell for two seasons had become the most talked-about attraction in theater business. Audiences were spellbound from one end of the country to the other. The simple staging had required little expenditure for production. On Broadway it had been an immense success in the midst of other lavish productions costing up to a quarter of a million dollars. The spoken word had finally come into its own, said many a commentator.

This freak staging, on top of the Laughton reading tours, inspired others to try likewise. So other "reading" programs, usually featuring a solo performer, and sometimes even a company, were launched. None of them, however, had more than a moderate success. Generally, they faded away, sometimes for sheer boredom, and again for lack of the spark that generates genuine excitement in the theater.

There were, to be sure, criticisms here and there. At Bushnell Memorial Hall in Hartford, five minutes after curtain time, an irate couple charged into the lobby from the auditorium almost shouting words to the effect that they had not bought tickets to an elocution lesson. Here and there such an innovation in stage art was sure to be misunderstood by a few.

The traveling was difficult; four dramatic stars of this caliber had not been pushed around the country on one-night stands for many a year. And there was occasional rebellion, especially from one—Charles Boyer. He was the source, also, of the most serious criticism of all—his accent produced a rash of complaint letters. But still they continued to buy tickets; and the same people came back for a second, third, and sometimes a fourth and even a fifth performance.

Producer Gregory was, therefore, confirmed in his decision to return the company to the road for a third tour. Not only was there remaining virgin territory to be played but many other spots could be revisited. In the following September, therefore, the final national tour of the same company was launched in Santa Barbara, California. It was not the same company for long, however, for Laughton soon dropped out, never to rejoin the cast, and was replaced by Vincent Price. No one in the cast was really sorry when the tour finally came to an end in the Civic Opera House in Chicago on December 15.

The gross receipts of *Don Juan* are of special interest for several reasons. Four actors, four high stools, four lecterns, and a black backdrop (the entire show) drew in two seasons over $1,500,000 in forty-six weeks of playing time. No long tour could be booked because of the prior commitments of the actors. So it was all done in bits: tour of seven weeks; two months off; four weeks in England; one month off; nine weeks tour, including one night at Carnegie Hall in New York; then five weeks at the Century Theater, New York; two months off;

eight weeks at the Plymouth Theater, New York; three months off; and then a final thirteen-week tour. It had cost less than $5,000 to get the show on the road in the beginning.

According to Sir Cedric Hardwicke, "The greatest strain that one actor can be put to is listening to another. Just as a tennis player will shoot the ball at you and get the thrill of making the right return, so we shoot lines at each other. Never for an instant since we started our tour have we been bored. We never try to defeat each other, of course – it is just the fun of inventing new readings and trying to give fresh meaning to the superb wit and wisdom of G.B.S."

In addition to having demonstrated the power and entertainment value of an old Shaw script, Paul Gregory was thereby established, now as a front-ranking producer. Some said he was just lucky, a momentary flash of genius; that Laughton had conceived and designed the production; and that such a phenomenal success could not be immediately repeated. But there were others to follow.

The effect on the respective careers of the First Drama Quartette was stimulating, to say the least. Charles Laughton's career was given renewed impetus. It was a crowning achievement to his attainments as an actor, and he acquired added reputation as a director. Agnes Moorehead was recognized more fully than ever for her fine acting talent. Sir Cedric Hardwicke gained new stature in his distinguished acting career. And finally, Charles Boyer, no longer in demand as the great screen lover, had proved conclusively the scope and power of his dramatic talent. Once a capable actor of diverse parts in Paris, he had become typed in Hollywood; now, his stage career was resumed. And collectively they had attained lasting fame at the summit of the theater hierarchy of great performances.

18

John Brown's Body

> *"Art has no nation—but the mortal sky*
> *Lingers like gold in immortality . . . .*
> *Receive the words that should have walked as bold*
> *As the storm walks along the mountain crest*
> *And are like beggars whining in the cold. . . .*
> *Armies of shadows and the shadow sound."*
> *—Stephen Vincent Benét*
> *(invocation to* John Brown's Body*)*

While visiting Paul Gregory in Hollywood during the summer of 1952, Dorothy and I were for the first time able to catch the spirit and momentum of the new producing enterprise firsthand. From one small back-room office, the spread of his activities now occupied a suite of five offices. Many new projects were in the air.

The most likely candidate for the next touring vehicle was *John Brown's Body*, an epic poem by Stephen Vincent Benét, which had reposed on library shelves for many years. This project became a certainty when Tyrone Power consented to head the company. After reading the book he became as excited about the prospect as Paul, who claimed to have nourished the idea ever since the power and drama of Benét's epic had first impressed itself upon him in high school days.

The first plan was to have it rendered to symphonic accompaniment. The cost of composing a score and sending out an orchestra to tour with the company, however, soon disposed of that idea. Paul finally settled for a chorus that would sing songs, give the bugle calls and battle cries, reproduce the tramping feet of armies, call the pigs, and represent other assorted noises. And so it happened that the Voices of Walter Schumann achieved starring status in a notable production.

To peruse the book of *John Brown's Body* from beginning to end required several hours of devoted reading. Cutting the poem to performance length was a prodigious task that finally became Laughton's assignment. After the King Herod chore in *Salome*, however, he was ready to take on almost anything. And time was of the essence with a new season coming on and star availabilities limited.

Laughton's working daily through hot July weeks by the side of his newly built pool (designed by his friend, Frank Lloyd Wright) accomplished the impossible. The book was broken down to essentials that emphasized the important dramatic sequences. Tyrone Power, representing romantic youth, was assigned to the portrayal of seventeen characters. Judith Anderson was engaged to represent the feminine point of view. And Raymond Massey, portraying the more mature characters, completed a stellar trio of talent that was to again make dramatic history under the Laughton–Gregory production banner.

It was very early on a chill October morning in the subsequent fall that another call came through from Paul Gregory in Hollywood, where the time was midnight. During the daylight hours Charles Laughton had been preparing the new production for touring, and at nights he was playing in *Don Juan in Hell* in the course of its two-week run at the Philharmonic Auditorium in Los Angeles. During the day of this call, Tyrone Power had acquired serious doubts about the future of *John Brown's Body* and decided to withdraw. Then, during the evening show, Laughton collapsed on the stage from sheer exhaustion.

This was the first real crisis since the tribulations attendant on the launching of *Don Juan in Hell*. And, to Paul it seemed as though his new world had suddenly collapsed around him. We had a heavy season of attractions booked which had just gotten under way. Nevertheless, it was immediately decided that Dorothy should take a plane to Hollywood the next day and lend a hand. She remained for two weeks, during which time Laughton was replaced by Vincent Price for the *Don Juan in Hell* tour and *John Brown's Body* became successfully launched with Tyrone Power.

The chorus of assorted noises was selected and trained by Walter Schumann, who also made the arrangements and composed original music. Billed as the Voices of Walter Schumann, it comprised a fourth starring element that lent added distinction to the production.

The staging of the show was also unique in its use of an "acting bar," suggested by Paul. This was a narrow cushioned board about eight feet long, supported at waist height, around which the three stars worked. This time they read without scripts, each one portraying his respective character while assuming various positions in front of, behind, and sometimes seated or reclining on the acting bar, or balustrade.

John Beaufort of the *Christian Science Monitor* designed a handsome full-page display based on drawings by Don Freeman. In the text he wrote,

> From the power and beauty of the poetic word, a new-old magic has been restored to the theater. Living people, real and imaginary, move through the imagination's third dimension. John Brown, Lincoln, Lee, dark slaves, white owners, soldiers of North and South and the women who love them.

Timed to coincide with the opening of the tour, *Collier's Magazine* carried a four-page color spread saying, "John Brown's Body Hits the Road—a notable cast tours with a no-set, no-costume version of Stephen Vincent Benét's great Civil War poem. It proves again that words alone can be box-office magic." In the accompanying story Evelyn Harvey wrote,

> Without visual aids, sound becomes the all-important factor, and chorus and principals toss the lines smoothly from one to the other. Judith Anderson leans forward into the mike and speaks:

"Out of his heart the chanting buildings rise—"

Then Tyrone Power continues:

"Rivet and girder, motor and dynamo—"

Next, Raymond Massey picks up the lines—

"Pillar of smoke by day and fire by night . . . ."

Life magazine also carried a four-page spread with the headline, "Poetic Platform Drama—Three Stars Make Stage Triumph of Benét's *John Brown's Body*."

One of the most distinguished dramatic pieces of this or any other era, *John Brown's Body* achieved further fame for the producers and reaped a harvest of press encomiums. That such literary material could be converted to stage purposes and presented with financial profit from one end of the country to the other had probably never occurred to anyone before—at least it had not been done in a big way. But the effect was far-reaching, and the attraction played extended tours throughout two seasons. These included a run on Broadway and a successful tour of the South.

For that matter, it could have continued playing but for the pressure on Tyrone Power's time. His earnings from motion pictures were so enormous that he could scarcely take prolonged leaves of absence. It is to this star's great credit that he would undertake a project of this character. Uncomplaining and cooperative, Tyrone was a model trouper. He accepted the hardships of traveling in the bus with the company, was considerate of the cast, gave brilliant press interviews, and was always gracious to the sponsors and the public.

It is said that today there is only one family that antedates that of Tyrone Power in theatrical history, and that is the many-branched Lupinos. The first Tyrone Power in the theater was born in 1795 and died in 1841. He was a victim of a shipwreck at the height of a distinguished career while en route home to England from his third successful American tour.

So our Tyrone Power, the fourth generation in a family of actors, came by his touring instincts naturally. His great ambition was to succeed on the stage as he had in movies and to follow in his father's footsteps as an actor of the first stature. It is also interesting to note that his father began playing in movies as early as 1914.

In discussing the *John Brown's Body* tours, Tyrone was once quoted in an interview to the effect that

> the actor must do his work on the road, touring the hinterlands, the provinces, the inland cities and towns of America, instead of sticking to Broadway, if he is to realize his full capabilities. You can get just as sedentary and stale in New York as you can in Hollywood doing the same thing night after night. Don't misunderstand me. I don't mean to belittle the importance of Broadway or the fine work being done in films; but I do feel strongly that an actor needs the stimulus of new audiences to continue doing his best work.
>
> Mine is not a rebellion against the movie industry but a reaching toward a fuller and richer career in the most personal sense of experiment and trial as an actor.

During the second season, Anne Baxter replaced Judith Anderson. This was not an easy assignment, but under Laughton's coaching, Anne delivered a first-rate performance. And she turned out to be an exceptionally good trouper during the entire twenty-week tour.

John Brown's Body proved in every way to be a worthy successor to *Don Juan in Hell*. It followed in the trail already blazed up and down and across the country—playing in auditoriums, theaters, concert halls, gymnasiums, field houses, and other out-of-the way places. It demonstrated further that great drama, effectively though simply presented, could attract and inspire large audiences.

It was at the beginning of the third season of touring Gregory attractions that the policy was adopted of equipping each company with complete sound, as well as lighting, equipment. This enabled both companies then performing to play in large-capacity facilities without the artistry of the production being jeopardized. Never before had purely dramatic productions, dependent largely on the speaking voice, been presented so successfully before huge audiences of up to eight thousand persons.

John Brown's Body eventually grossed close to $1,500,000.

Among other benefits, it sparked a revival of interest in Stephen Vincent Benét's great works. And the author's widow drew an unexpected windfall in royalties at a time when the works of only a few poets were remunerative. But it had required talent of the highest order in every department to take this poetry and transform it into stage entertainment. Thus it achieved success in a medium that must have been quite far from its author's original intention.

Of all the tours I have handled, this piece has remained my favorite. Its unique staging, with the talented Schumann chorus giving out its assorted noises, made it a memorable presentation. Although the first tour had lost heavily ($58,000), the show went well into the black on its second national tour.

19

The Caine Mutiny Court Martial

> "An officer relieving his
> commanding officer or
> recommending such action
> together with all others who
> so counsel, must bear the
> legitimate responsibility
> for, and must be prepared
> to justify such action."
> —Navy Regulations, Article 186

By the spring of 1953, Paul Gregory had three seasons of *Don Juan in Hell* behind him and one of *John Brown's Body*. Although the touring possibilities of the first had not been exhausted, the company had had enough, and there were no substitutes available of comparable stature. After some urging, producer Gregory agreed to chance another tour for the latter. But a new attraction was needed to keep the operation in full swing.

The Caine Mutiny Court Martial was determined to open in the early fall of 1953. Staged more conventionally, this production differed from its predecessors for that very reason. The element of simplicity, however, was retained in the stage setting—only a set of plain beige draperies for background. In addition to the judge's bench, there were the witness chair and a few plain courtroom furnishings.

The press saw still another reading in the offing and so announced the new production. Thereby a minor tempest was set off in the Gregory office, which may have been one reason why he decided to shift his stance and be conventional for a change. Hollywood loves to type producers as well as actors, but this one did not conform to any given mold.

The original *Caine Mutiny* book, a best-seller by Herman Wouk, had previously been sold for motion picture production. There was, however, nothing in the movie contract to preclude the sale of concert rights to a small portion of the book. In fact, while the movie script was shooting during the summer of 1953, I was booking a tour for a stage production for which the script was yet to be written. Fortunately, it was to be another year before the picture could be released.

It was while thumbing at random through the pages of the novel one day that producer Gregory came by chance upon the court martial scene. He was so fascinated by its high drama that he could not wait to procure the rights for stage production. As it turned out, this became a joint venture with author Herman Wouk.

Although Herman Wouk was not to deliver a playing script until June 15, a letter announcement over Paul's signature was mailed to potential sponsors across the country under the date of May 14. At this point, therefore, all I had to offer to sponsors was a potential play to star John Hodiak and Henry Fonda. By working through the summer, I was able to book a substantial tour to open October 12 in Santa Barbara with a Broadway opening in the offing for the following January.

In the meantime, the script did not come June 15 nor did it come by July 15. Then August 1 came and no script. Finally, it arrived two months late and an hour too long in reading time. Author Wouk came to California to huddle with stagecraftsman Laughton. This was a trying process, and the author finally returned to New York, leaving the entire pruning and surgery in Laughton's hands with carte blanche to delete, alter, or add verbiage wherever he should choose.

Originally, it was expected that the new stage show would be directed by Henry Fonda, but he was eventually cast for Lieutenant Greenwald, lawyer for the defendant. The part of

Lieutenant Maryk was assigned to John Hodiak. The other starring role of Captain Queeg became a real problem. Many were considered, but Lloyd Nolan was finally selected. Long a fine actor, Lloyd somehow had never had just the right chance to show his mettle. But Captain Queeg was to put him on the top rung and gain the Donaldson Award for the best acting performance of the season on Broadway. Subsequently, he received an Emmy for the best acting performance of 1955 by reason of his splendid performance in the role on TV.

The dramatic challenge of playing Captain Queeg, who was already familiar to millions of readers, appealed to Lloyd Nolan. During rehearsals he remarked, "I've never drawn the line at any type or portrayal. All I ask is that the part afford me a chance to be creative. Gangsters, staunch heads of crime bureaus, detectives, policemen—I've played them all. But Captain Queeg is as tough a role as I've ever tackled, and I'm loving the tussle."

Other cast selections were also fortunate. The all-male company, even the "silent six" who served on the judge's bench (one of them was James Garner), were all excellent. What was not so fortunate was the engagement of a well-known movie director to stage the play. It was thought that the play required a documentary style of direction, for which he would be particularly well suited, but he seemed to be unable to direct within the framework of stage limitations. Complaints from members of the company forced the issue, and he was replaced by Charles Laughton with only ten days remaining before the opening date.

As usual, everything was done according to formula and otherwise to make this another production attractive to the public. The play derived most of its title from a best-selling book; it had a name director; the cast was headed by three star players; and, lastly, it carried the label, "A Paul Gregory–Charles Laughton Production."

No one can ever feel comfortable, however, until ticket sales begin to justify the faith and effort that has been put into a production. The first sale to set off sparks was in Stockton, California. This was an important landmark, indeed. A telephone report from the local sponsor there brought the first news of the rush for tickets. Everyone was promptly cheered from their preopening depressions. And it was not long before similar reports followed from other cities.

Except for Claremont and Stockton, the performances in ten other California cities, plus the week's engagement in San Francisco, were presented and managed by Dorothy. She rolled up gross ticket receipts overall of $96,182 to send the company out on the road with a profitable start. Furthermore, the press and public reactions left nothing to be desired. This show also effectively disposed of the reading label that had been attached to the previous Gregory–Laughton efforts.

En route to the East, *The Caine Mutiny Court Martial* was booked into the huge field house of Oklahoma State University in Stillwater with the stipulation that no more than four thousand tickets were to be sold. The company arrived to find that twice that number had been sold. The show went on, nevertheless, with no complaints.

In charge of the show on tour was a seasoned company manager who, in a short time, went completely haywire. In Dallas, he lost or misplaced three thousand dollars worth of railroad tickets (weeks later they arrived in the mail at the Hollywood office). Then, in Kansas City he posted a notice to the effect that the company would play the next night in Portland, Maine, disregarding the regular itinerary. This brought forth an irate telephone call from Fonda at midnight that got producer Gregory out of bed for no good reason at all. En route in the bus to Chicago, said manager struck one of the actors. It seemed that this manager always kept to himself, but some of the younger talent couldn't resist occasional attempts to get a reaction from him by coming up from behind and snapping his ear or dislodging his hat—all in fun. Then in Chicago he was nearly three hundred dollars short on the box-office settlement. So it became obvious that a replacement would have to be made.

Paul, accompanied by Dorothy, went to Chicago to discharge the erring manager, and I was called from New York to check him out and take over the company. The engagement at the

Civic Opera House in Chicago was a huge success. Even the redoubtable Claudia Cassidy came out with fulsome praise, and then she wrote a follow-up story that was almost unprecedented.

With Chicago safely in the bag, I proceeded with the tour until a new company manager could be secured. Then Dorothy and Paul followed the *Caine Mutiny Court Martial* company to Rockton, Illinois, where they all put up at the famed Wagon Wheel Inn. It was a frosty Thanksgiving eve. The countryside was white with the season's first snowfall, and the roads were slick. Following the evening's performance before a packed and enthusiastic house in nearby Beloit, the cast returned to the inn for a midnight feast as guests of their producer. The turkeys were brought in by a train of waiters with due ceremony, and the occasion was festive indeed. After the feasting, actors Nolan, Fonda, and Hodiak each entertained with an appropriate sample of his histrionic ability. It was in every way a delightful occasion—one of those interludes in the hectic theatrical pace that always provides a happy memory.

In the East, I also presented the performances in those cities wherein I had been customarily operating—White Plains, Greenwich, Hartford, Boston, Newark, and Washington. No one ever wants the week before Christmas, so I took the Boston Opera House and grossed over $30,000 in four days. This record take was to be exceeded three weeks later in Washington, D.C., when my partner, Irvin Feld, and I paid the Gregory office $19,443 out of gross ticket receipts of $29,912 for three performances in two days. This was an all-time high for a purely box-office take on a straight dramatic attraction. Also, these figures do not include the 20 percent admissions taxes, which could be legitimately included as part of the sales prices of the tickets.

A week later, on January 18, the *Caine Mutiny Court Martial* opened at the Plymouth Theater on Broadway with an advance sale estimated at well over five hundred thousand dollars and 100 percent press raves.

The Caine Mutiny Court Martial turns out to be as expert as everyone had hoped. Staged and played with the greatest ease and sincerity, it tells a shattering tale softly . . . . In his velvety style of staging Charles Laughton has given it the perfect performance.

—Brooks Atkinson, *New York Times*

The Caine Mutiny Court Martial is a theatrical adventure which builds to a second-act climax of such hair-raising intensity that you are sure nothing, and no one, can ever top it. . . . It is a thrilling achievement.

—Walter F. Kerr, New York *Herald Tribune*

This play is a new creation for the theater, with the theater, and by the theater—and it is enormously compelling and exciting. It is the modern stage at its best.

—John Chapman, New York *Daily News*

Caine Mutiny Provides Magnificent Theater—So we suggest that you rush to the box office immediately, if you hope to see it in the future. And see it you must. For this is an arresting, absorbing, and completely fascinating evening of theater.

—Robert Coleman, New York *Daily Mirror*

It can probably remain here until the performers are honorably retired from the Navy. It is merely a magnificent success.

—John C. McClain, New York *Journal American*

Although Charles Laughton had taken over direction of the play on short notice, he had received no direct compensation, not to mention program and billing credit. His was a tremendous contribution not only in helping to make a play out of the first bulky script but also in whipping the last few days of rehearsal into a compelling stage piece.

So in the week remaining prior to opening in New York, Laughton's name was substituted on all billing and credits. And the weekly stipend was thereafter continued in his name—only simple justice, after all. Although the play was a solid hit on Broadway for over a year, it was prematurely closed. Such procedure while a play is still making a profit was, to say the least, unorthodox. But that was just another of the Gregory "imponderables." Both Laughton and Gregory had lost interest in the *Caine Mutiny Court Martial*. Early in December a closing date had been discussed with me and press agent Karl Bernstein in New York, but it was to be many weeks hence. Then the producers went off to Jamaica where the sun and tides must have induced them to relinquish the cares of the show immediately. Without consulting anyone, they sent word to close the show. The company as well as the Shuberts were caught unprepared, and when a telephone call was put through to Jamaica, the operator reported that Charles Laughton and Paul Gregory were "on the beach and not to be disturbed."

Dorothy and the Shuberts agreed to keep the show open another week anyway. Another producer took over the attraction and continued the New York engagement for several weeks. The show was then taken to Chicago. After a successful run, it played a big week in St. Louis and finally a six-week run at the Huntington Hartford Theater in Los Angeles — all under the aegis of another management.

After the original company had been successfully launched, it was inevitable that there would be another road tour, so a new company was formed to go out in the midsummer of 1954. Heading the cast were Paul Douglas as Captain Queeg; Wendell Corey as Lieutenant Greenwald; and Steve Brodie as Lieutenant Maryk. Producer Gregory prepared the company, and Laughton polished off the final rehearsals. A thirty-seven-week tour was booked — mostly concert-type appearances, with occasional theater engagements. It opened in June in San Francisco and proceeded next to Central City, where four sold-out weeks were played in the famed old Opera House.

From here the tour proceeded in a succession of one-night stands, occasionally interspersed with a week's stand in the larger cities. As was inevitable, petty frictions and jealousies developed. The stars became irritable, suffered imaginary wrongs, and made dire threats to their producer until it was obvious they were doing him a favor to continue accepting their large weekly stipends. Two of them had never earned that kind of money in a stage piece, and their reputations were being considerably enhanced at the same time.

166

The third, Paul Douglas, was the most miserable of all, in spite of a great personal success. Too long he had been separated from home and his charming Jan Sterling. So it was after the performance on a Saturday evening late in January 1955 that he gave vent to the famous outburst that was to hit the press in screaming headlines from coast to coast. On being accosted by an Associated Press reporter with the question, "Well, how do you like the South, Mr. Douglas?" he snapped, "The South stinks — it is full of segregation and sow belly." And there was more unforgivable language.

Most of the remainder of the tour had been booked across the South and into Texas. Tickets soon became impossible to sell and, although a few engagements would not have been affected, to avoid serious losses to local sponsors it was deemed best to close the show. Seven weeks were canceled. I planed to Chicago in an effort to persuade the original touring company, now playing in the Blackstone Theater, to pick up at least some of the canceled time, but they would have none of it. Eventually, it became necessary to produce and send out a third company, which picked up most of the lost dates. Principal star of this company was William Bendix, who also gave a good performance as Captain Queeg. Unfortunately, it was difficult to pick up the lost momentum, and business was somewhat below the accustomed level.

The Douglas episode led to more bad feeling. Various versions of the affair appeared in the press, and attempted explanations proved of no avail. The matter before long came to the desk of Ed Russell, veteran actor and West Coast representative of the Actors' Equity Association. Without fear or favor, he conducted honest hearings, which finally led to a condemnation of the actor's conduct by the Equity Council in New York. They placed him on probation for the period of a year

Although Equity had made every effort to have calm, fair judgments prevail, Douglas filed a suit against his producer for one million dollars. Gregory, however, withheld filing of a damage suit in favor of arbitration proceedings, as originally requested of both sides by Angus Duncan, administrator for Actors' Equity in New York. Eventually Douglas agreed to

167

make a substantial payment in settlement of the claims, so actions on both sides were thereby liquidated.

In 107 weeks of playing, *Caine Mutiny Court Martial* racked up gross receipts aggregating more than three million dollars. And a notable addition had been made to America's literature of the drama.

20

Three for Tonight

"There is no substitute for talent"
wrote Aldous Huxley.
"Like Portia's quality of mercy—
'It droppeth as the gentle rain from heaven
Upon the place beneath; it is twice bless'd;
It blesses him that gives and him that takes.' "
It is the magnet that draws
us, the shimmering white
light that burns in a
performance. . . . Whatever
its surroundings, talent is the
divine spark in the human situation.
—John Beaufort, the
Christian Science Monitor

In our twentieth-concert season of 1952–1953 in West-chester, Dorothy and I included both a return engagement of *Don Juan in Hell* and the new Gregory show, *John Brown's Body.* Season concert subscriptions, however, had continued to show a steady decrease. The new emphasis was on special events. The regular subscription season closed in March 1953 with the Robert Shaw Chorale, which only added another twelve hundred dollars to the season's deficit. So it was decided not to contract for a new season of attractions.

Clearly the old subscription formula was dead. The days of great recital artists were mostly history. The customers were buying shows, ballets, novelties—ensemble attractions. In my capacity as eastern representative for Gregory Associates, Inc., most of my time was being devoted to booking. There was not only a second tour to be made for *John Brown's Body* but also a new show to route.

Christmas was to be our last in the beautiful Westchester home at Armonk Village. Dorothy returned to California to become Paul's "right arm." The house was sold, and I followed to California with the car and personal effects. As of January 1, 1954, Paul and I set up the Gregory Booking Office as a Division of Gregory Associates, Inc. A second company of *Caine Mutiny Court Martial* had to be booked for the road. And then there was to be another theatrical baby introduced to the public.

As one writer observed, *Three for Tonight* was to make it four in a row for what was becoming an impressive array of stage productions under the Gregory–Laughton label. This one, however, came by the caesarian process. It was an unruly infant from the time it first drew breath until finally laid to rest a year later at the height of its tortured career.

This one began with the Champions—Marge and Gower. So impressive were they in an hour's telecast on Ed Sullivan's "Toast of the Town" that Paul had taken them under contract in the spring of 1953 for a concert tour. Nearly a year later it became necessary to do something about it, but no format suggested itself. The Champions had evidently thought of the program as being built around primarily their work. When it finally came down to cases, the producer decided that more variety must be added to the presentation even if another star had to be secured. This created a temporary impasse, and for a time it appeared there would be no show at all. But the upshot resulted in three starring elements—the Champions, Harry Belafonte, and the Voices of Walter Schumann.

Belafonte's inclusion in the cast was by way of the Dutch Treat Club in New York. While a guest at one of its regular Tuesday luncheon meetings, I first heard Harry Belafonte—a guest performer on the weekly program. I was sufficiently impressed to send producer Gregory (who was abroad) a cable that here was the missing element needed to round out the cast of the new musical. Gregory met Belafonte on his return to New York. They promptly became friends, and the new talent was soon under contract to his new producer.

In the meantime, I had already booked a tour, largely on the strength across the country of the Gregory name. Contracts read "Marge and Gower Champion and a third star to be announced." The Champions had enjoyed night club successes and had played some parts in movies. In arranging the bookings, I found that they seemed to be known only in some of the larger cities. Belafonte's name was even less well known. From association with the two tours of *John Brown's Body*, the Voices of Walter Schumann, however, had become favorably known to leading managers and their public from coast to coast.

The writer brought in to do the job of welding the talent into a coherent evening's entertainment was not up to the occasion. The task of devising a format fell back onto Paul, but it was Gower Champion whose stage direction did much to unify the pieces of the puzzle and give the performance meaning and continuity. In fact, to the inventiveness and taste displayed in his choreography and the skill of his direction must be given the credit for finally evolving a sparkling stage show.

Three for Tonight was finally launched in San Diego under Dorothy's management. The audience loved the show, but unfortunately the reviewer for the San Diego *Union* failed to be impressed. Again, it was an entirely different type of production from its predecessor. But the show had the necessary spark and production quality that was unmistakable. Other performances presented by Dorothy followed in several California cities, including the Alcazar Theater in San Francisco, where thousands were being turned away when the run had to be concluded because of tour commitments.

Here was a stunning entertainment attraction in the modern manner. Dance, song, and drama were welded together by young professional talent in a manner to make this a standout concert event. The significance of the production as an answer to changing public taste lay in the new format that combined in a single deftly arranged program such a variety of performing talent.

The tour, however, was to meet with a succession of snags. There were times when Belafonte stole the reviews. Although the stars were being thoroughly well paid, they were unhappy; and the producer's margin was always so narrow that any unusual circumstance could reduce it to the vanishing point.

Then Marge Champion became ill in St. Louis, and three sold-out performances were missed, causing a considerable loss. Finally, it became necessary to cancel the last three weeks of the tour's playing time so that she could rest and get into shape for the Broadway opening in April. Through Dorothy's diligence in setting up theater parties, advance sales in New York were considerable and insured at least a limited run.

These cancellations fell at almost the identical time that Paul Douglas blew his top and caused the closing of the touring *Caine Mutiny Court Martial* company. For the first time in five years, these were not just a few cancellations; there were a total of ten weeks of playing time. Between the two shows, over forty-five cities were involved. No matter how valid the reasons, everyone lost—even the actors this time. Most of the local engagements, however, were subsequently made good.

Broadway reviewers gave producer Gregory another set of glowing notices:

> Producer Paul Gregory doesn't need 3 for Tonight so long as he's got Harry Belafonte for tonight. Marge and Gower Champion are just about perfect for the light, graceful, ingratiating chores they have been called upon to do.
> — Walter E. Kerr, New York *Herald-Tribune*

> Harry Belafonte is magnificent . . . triumphant. Marge and Gower Champion come bearing dances in many moods, all of them attractive . . . the new show is original and delightful.
> — Brooks Atkinson, *New York Times*

> 3 For Tonight . . . is not theater in the sense that any effort has been made toward formalized settings. . . . But it is really great . . ., the talent is enormous, this is an unquestioned hit.
> — John McClain, New York *Journal American*

By this time the three stars' salaries had mounted to $9,000 per week. Business had to be capacity to give the production even a small margin. With summer coming on and Belafonte's agent demanding still more coin when his contract came up for renewal on July 1, it was decided to close the Broadway run.

Now receiving a salary of $4,000 per week, at the age of twenty-six Belafonte was struggling to get along owing to financial involvements. He was, therefore, supplementing his income by playing midnight shows at nightclubs in New Jersey and Manhattan. He would reach the Plymouth Theater with a voice husky and strained from the exertions of the night before. Occasionally some of his numbers even had to be omitted, which was hardly fair to the show that had now brought him national fame.

The Champions were not too happy with their assignments. *Three for Tonight* gave them their best vehicle to date and, for the first time, showed this delightful and talented pair of entertainers in person to large audiences across the country. Their costumes cost somewhat more than was necessary; several thousand dollars was expended in literary material ordered but never written or even used; and a special dance floor was carried on tour that had to be laid down at every performance, a luxury not even permitted to star ballet performers on tour.

If the attraction had achieved nothing else, however, it uncovered to national view for the first time a new major talent in Belafonte. He had been knocking at the gates to fame and fortune for years, guided by the faithful Jack Rollins, until Gregory's show provided the key. From then on his rise was phenomenal. A scant two years later his annual earnings had to be expressed in seven figures. His weekly salary in *Three for Tonight* had climbed from $2,500 at the outset to $4,000; and when his contract was up for renewal and his agent increased the stipend to $7,500, Gregory decided he could not afford to keep the show open. But it was this first national tour that finally launched Harry Belafonte into the big time.

Thus, the checkered career of *Three for Tonight* came to a close on July 3 — the first Gregory show to do so after only a single season of playing, although I had already laid out a tour for the subsequent season. Also, for the first time I was compelled to finally notify the many local sponsors across the country that there would be no Gregory stage show in the ensuing season. So many refused to believe it that I was kept busy for a time placating the disappointed managers. Some of them still refused to believe it and announced the annual Gregory show regardless. The result was booming ticket sales for several mythical Gregory performances—titles to be announced.

The tour concluded with a week's engagement at the Greek Theater in Hollywood, where the gross intake was $85,402 in seven performances—a record-breaking figure up to that time for a week's engagement on the West Coast. This was the first of the Gregory stage shows to gross less than a million dollars, although the total intake was close.

21

The Night of the Hunter

*"I make pictures to
entertain audiences
and at the same time to
give them spiritual uplift.*
—Frank Capra, November 6, 1971

During the interval in Chicago when I met with Paul
Gregory to be on hand for the engagement of *The Caine Mutiny
Court Martial* at the Civic Opera House, another project came
up and received the blessing of all on hand.

Dorothy was bursting with news of an exciting new book that
Paul proposed to make into a motion picture. In galley form I
read *The Night of the Hunter* at one sitting and agreed with the
others on its potential. Upon publication the book was to
become a best-seller and, eventually, the first motion picture
produced by Paul Gregory and directed by Charles Laughton.

The following morning I was off with the company to
Milwaukee, having had to take over the company from the
manager who had gone berserk. Dorothy and Paul set off in the
opposite direction—Hollywood—to start work on *The Night of
the Hunter*.

From time to time, Paul had had overtures from certain of the
leading studios to become a motion picture producer. There is,
however, a right time for everything, and so far he had not

allowed himself to be lured out of bounds by various and sundry offers. It was important that he retain control of his production with a right to the final editing. And there was the little matter of financing. The intricacies and "angles" involved in the financing, producing, and distributing of a major motion picture are quite beyond anything so far devised in the legitimate field.

After studying several studio propositions, Paul finally decided on the United Artists deal as a setup in which he would feel the most congenial. And it appeared to assure the most independence. Once the project had been tossed into the hopper, however, he was to find himself in a straitjacket.

The late James Agee, of *African Queen* fame, was commissioned to do the script. Much of the summer of 1954 was spent in this task of adaptation and rewriting—all done in close collaboration with Laughton. In the meantime, Paul set about the work of casting, for which he had demonstrated a consistent knack. After the picture was well into production only one replacement became necessary.

Selected for the starring role of the phony preacher was Robert Mitchum. Shelley Winters, a one-time pupil of Laughton's classes, played the preacher's wife. Other important roles were assigned to Billy Chapin (child star); Jimmy Gleason; Evelyn Varden; and, by no means least, Lillian Gish. For the last named it marked the great actress's return to Hollywood after an absence of over seven years.

At one time during the filming, Billy Chapin was suddenly stricken with appendicitis. At the rate of nearly twenty thousand dollars a day, work had to be suspended—fortunately for only a few days. It was veteran Lillian Gish, however, who showed a real understanding of what was happening to producer Gregory's budget, to which he was being rigidly held by United Artists' auditors. In a telephone call, she offered to forego her fee if it would help matters. This was sunshine, indeed, coming through the clouds, but fortunately the emergency was met with additional financing. The picture finally ran only $150,000 over budget.

Laughton assumed carte blanche authority and became lord of the proceedings. Even producer Gregory had to tiptoe unobtrusively through the shadows onto the set if he wanted to watch any of the takes, so as not to disturb the master's mood. And Laughton always did have difficulty conforming his perfectionist tendencies to time schedules. The net result was that a good picture somehow fell short of realizing its potential to become an outstanding picture.

Dorothy served as the producer's general assistant throughout. Her facility for statistics and analyzing charts and reports was of inestimable help. And she was thrilled with watching the whole process of turning a story from galley form to script to the finished product recorded and edited on film.

Dorothy had the hundreds of reviews coming in from all over the world analyzed. She reported that over 80 percent were favorable notices, many of them excellent. Only a very few were bad. There are many ways by which one can account for an unwarranted criticism of good entertainment. More often than not it may be the result of the writer's personal dislike or hatred of someone prominently identified with the show. And then some papers have a deliberate policy of destructive criticism, thinking thereby to arouse controversy and so increase circulation.

Dorothy's part in the picture making relieved the producer of much executive detail. She read and analyzed the several weekly reports from the studio; kept a weather eye on the budget; checked on the publicity and promotion campaign; and at all times was at producer Gregory's elbow to assist and advise on the day-to-day problems.

Night of the Hunter was good entertainment, to say the least, and its occasional revivals on TV testify to its durability as such.

22

Triple Television Triumph

"Television is not going to hurt this 2,000 year old darling—it will remain the Rembrandt of show business. . . It is not going to change human nature."
—Billy Rose

Before the end of his first five years as an entrepreneur in show business, Paul Gregory was to achieve status in the third field (after radio and movies) of modern mass entertainment— television production. Having had overtures from the top television systems from time to time, he decided now to discover for himself what this new monster of the show world had to offer.

Paul signed to do three programs for the Ford Star Jubilee, one of the top-ranking monthly spots on the Columbia Broadcasting System. The first of these took place in June, immediately following the close of the *Three for Tonight* run on Broadway. This was the first time that a show was to be moved directly from its New York theater engagement to a television studio. Although redirected from a two-and-a-quarter-hour stage show down to an hour-and-a-half TV performance, it lost nothing of its spontaneity and charm.

On returning to Hollywood, Paul was met at International Airport by Dorothy and me. He had little to say immediately about TV and looked haggard and disgusted.

"Never," he vowed, "will I do another TV program. The producer is nobody. The whole thing is a clock-watching job run by sullen, uninspired technicians who know little about stage art and care a whole lot less." And—the final blow— although the budget had appeared generous, there was nothing left for producer Gregory at payoff time. He was working for prestige and experience.

So, at that low moment, he was off the new medium forever and ever. This suited me fine, for it would get his mind back to the production of stage shows. I had been waiting for the green light on the next live show to go out on the road. In fact, it now seemed that Paul's first encounter with both TV and movies would definitely channel his thinking back along the lines of his several stage successes.

The embers of *The Caine Mutiny Court Martial* and its praises were still glowing; so before they turned to cold ashes, it was determined to take it before the TV cameras on November 11. The original cast was reassembled, and a top director, Franklin Shaffner, was secured. He and Paul cut the script to size. Although with a cast so well prepared only a week or ten days of rehearsal time would ordinarily have been used, Paul determined on a three-week period to insure success.

This time Dorothy was to be on hand again with her budget. After studying the inordinate union demands on rehearsals, she warned that costs were going to get out of hand. Through the intercession of Paul's TV representative in New York City, more adequate provisions were made, and Columbia assumed the unusual below-the-line costs. Everything looked more than auspicious this time. As rehearsals were about to start, however, the telephone one morning was ringing persistently as Dorothy entered the office. A friend was calling to report the sudden and untimely demise of smiling John Hodiak. So the original star cast would not be on hand after all. The unfortunate news was relayed to Paul in New York City, and Frank Lovejoy was soon engaged as replacement.

179

Hodiak's genial and infectious spirit was greatly missed. Charles Laughton, who narrated the hour-and-a-half TV program, paid him a fine tribute at the end. The performance itself was considered as close to perfection as any production in the dramatic field had been up to this time. In fact, as more time for appraisal elapsed, and criticisms, comments, and ratings were analyzed, there was no doubt that it had been the outstanding achievement of the season.

Ratings of other key programs at the time were pushed down several points below their usual levels. Had there been any tangible award for the year's top achievement in a dramatic show on TV, there is no question that it would have gone to "The Caine Mutiny Court Martial." As it was, the year's top acting achievement for a male star was voted to Lloyd Nolan, who delivered a magnificent performance.

Subsequently, Paul Gregory was given the Look TV Award for Best Dramatic Show — 1956.

Paul could not have desired anything more. This time the financial results would have been rewarding, except that William Goldman had tied up the net proceeds, as will be elaborated upon in the ensuing chapter. Paul was advised that he had three alternatives: produce independently under a new entity with no entanglements; leave the country for three years and produce elsewhere; or muddle through and try to capitalize as best he could on his accomplishments to date.

Paul chose the latter as the more logical course, his movie and stage production activities having been definitely stalemated. Goldman's lawyers were standing by to impound the earnings. So, he made every effort to postpone his third TV program until the legal skies cleared, but CBS wanted the third program as per contract.

For his third effort on TV, which was to be in the following February, it was decided to adapt Jim Bishop's best-selling book *"The Day Lincoln Was Shot."* Attracted by the intense drama of the book at the time of its publication, Paul was encouraged by Dorothy to go on with it. CBS was determined to produce the show on Saturday, February 11, on the eve of Lincoln's birthday anniversary, although the actual anniversary of Lincoln's death would have fallen two months later.

A writer was secured, who developed a script that became too involved for practical story telling. Three weeks ahead of the play date this script was laid aside, and Dennis and Terry Saunders were commissioned to begin writing another script. This they did in competent fashion—working literally day and night. After all, a lot of dialogue has to be written to occupy an hour and a half of playing time. And, while pages of the new script were still being turned out by typists, the earlier pages were being put into rehearsal ten days ahead of the actual performance.

Lillian Gish as Mary Todd Lincoln turned in a superb performance. Jack Lemmon as John Wilkes Booth was an effective villain. And Raymond Massey as Lincoln was competent. Paul had had other ideas on the casting for Lincoln, but the agency handling the Ford account insisted on Massey in spite of his $21,000 fee.

The opening scene, in particular, was memorable. Can one ever forget the great, rangy, slightly stooped figure of Lincoln as he strode from a distance down the length of a timeless corridor, heedless of curtains flapping at intervals, while a rose-tinted aura of light gave an eerie glow to this beautifully conceived prologue?

Directed by Delbert Mann, the production of this program was a masterpiece of organization. Elaborate sets for the many scenes were built around the sides and in every open spot in two huge adjoining rooms of CBS Television City. Overhead hung a fortune in lighting equipment that could be moved on tracks to any position.

During the performance, Mann's position was at a long counter in the control room while on either side sat two technicians. The whole was directed and controlled as a general would order and move around component parts of his army on a field of maneuvers.

Months later, when the returns for the season were all in, two of Paul Gregory's first three TV programs were listed in the accepted trade ratings as among the ten most-watched programs for the year. These were *The Caine Mutiny Court Martial* and *The Day Lincoln Was Shot*.

Paul's fourth television spectacular proved his undoing for the time being in that medium. The first three "specs" had been conformed to TV from established properties. This time he was to create, assemble, and present a sort of rundown on modern music. Ample funds and a galaxy of star talent were placed at his disposal by CBS. But Paul came up with a format that was flat and uninspired, and Leslie Stevens's script did not serve to improve matters.

The result was something called "Crescendo." It was set to open the new 1959 fall series of DuPont spectaculars — challenge enough in itself. But the results were unfortunate indeed and terminated Paul's activity on TV for some years to come.

23

Litigation and Liquidation

> *"Although doctors tell us
> that there are only four
> blood types in the human
> race, I am sure some day
> they will discover a fifth,
> a compound of showman's
> blood. It makes for a race apart."*
> —Louis Nizer in My Life In Court.

After the first flush of success with *Don Juan in Hell,* money
ceased to be a problem—at least for the time being. Starting
from scratch it had required hard work on Paul Gregory's part
to support even a modest office while sending Charles Laughton
out to do his inimitable readings before clubs, colleges, and
other organizations all over the country. The fees for these first
appearances ranged anywhere from three hundred dollars to
whatever the traffic would bear. Ultimately, Laughton's tours
developed into a five-month solid itinerary that was to bring
him an average of fifteen hundred dollars for each appearance.

When *Don Juan in Hell* arrived on Broadway, it was already
paid for as a production. Simply staged, there were no costumes
to buy (except a one-thousand-dollar gown for Agnes), and the
men wore their dinner jackets. And there was no production to
be built. As each subsequent stage show arrived in New York,

the same could be said. No money had to be raised, and each show was self-sufficient. Even the more conventional *Caine Mutiny Court Martial* was simply staged, with special draperies instead of the usual canvas stage set.

This enabled the performances to be given under any and all sorts of conditions—in gymnasiums, college field houses, regular theaters, etc. In fact, it was a feature of the Gregory–Laughton credo that their performances should be made available in out-of-the-way places, and heavy productions to travel would have been incompatible with their policy. The emphasis was rather on talent and literary content.

It was early realized that promotion on a national scale, particularly in the press, was important. In fact, it was impressed on young producer Gregory by advisors that he must hire a top press agent to build the Gregory name and, therefore, help to pave the way for the reception of succeeding productions across the country. And to accomplish this, he was told further that the one man to do the job was Russell Birdwell.

Not only had Birdwell masterminded three or four successful national campaigns on behalf of new picture releases (including *Gone with the Wind*) but he was supposed to be the open sesame to studio executives as well as the wise counselor in the ways of Hollywood and how to get ahead.

It required nearly two years of experience, however, before matters were to come to a head. Dorothy remembered well the check for $500 going out week after week for scanty services, wondering just how long this could be kept up.

Among other things, it was part of his job to prepare press books for the touring stage shows. Nothing was done until Dorothy's California dates on the *Caine Mutiny Court Martial* were only a few weeks away and there was no press material prepared. She wrote a long letter calling him to account and outlining the material needed. This letter was to figure later on in the trial.

Depending on Birdwell to open the doors, Paul could not understand why he was so slow in doing so. Birdwell, however, apparently lacked the entrees or else was loathe to use them. After he fouled up appointments in New York City with certain studio executives, his attitude was so defiant that he was sent a telegram of dismissal.

This step eventuated in a law suit whereby Birdwell claimed a five-year verbal contract with Gregory and an unlimited 5 percent of the producer's earnings, amounting to a sum well in excess of three hundred thousand dollars. Gregory Associates, Inc., was ably represented by Attorney Loyd Wright. At the resulting trial in the supreme court, not only was Birdwell unable to prove a contract (there was none, although it had once been discussed) but he collected no damages—only the weekly payments to the time of his dismissal, which Gregory had expected to pay in any case. One of the lessons that must be learned in Hollywood is to be wary in even discussing employment. Many people have been sued on the pretext that someone had been hired.

Although there had been other inordinate demands and legal skirmishes (reported elsewhere), the Birdwell case was to be only the curtain raiser for worse to come later in the year of 1955. The consequences were to be severe—the most serious was the suspension of Paul's producing activity. And it meant, among other things, no stage show launched for the season (1955–1956) for the first time in five years.

Offers of outside investment in the Laughton–Gregory productions had been received from time to time, but the first financing accepted was for *The Night of the Hunter*, which required nearly one million dollars. Of several picture projects, under consideration, Gregory selected *The Naked and the Dead* for his next effort. Two major studios had tried in vain to make a workable script from Norman Mailer's best-selling novel. Laughton had declared, however, that he knew the answer.

It was estimated roughly that this one would require anywhere from two to three million dollars to produce. Although United Artists had indicated its interest and willingness to go ahead with his next picture, Paul was not so ready, in view of his previous experience with this factory operation.

At least four of the major studios were also interested, and, from time to time, overtures had been received from a William Goldman on the other side of the continent in Philadelphia. An important motion picture exhibitor in the East, he wanted to enter production, and Paul was to be the means to this end.

Goldman and Gregory had never met, but some negotiations had been carried on through a Hollywood attorney known to both. The time finally arrived when either an end would have to be made to Goldman's overtures or else producer Gregory would have to get on a plane and fly to Philadelphia the next convenient weekend to see what it was all about.

On a Friday early in 1954, Paul flew to Philadelphia. That same night he was lavishly entertained on the roof of the Warwick Hotel, of which Goldman was part owner. Important guests included figures in the motion picture industry and civic leaders. Excellent food and liquors were served in liberal quantities, and flash bulbs popped, all providing a gala atmosphere in which almost anything could happen. Never before had Paul taken a major step hastily, without taking time out to study the implications. But this time he signed a memorandum agreement, within hours of his arrival, that encompassed all his future producing activities.

At midnight he telephoned the news to the astonished Olneys in Hollywood. This whole occasion would appear to mark the culmination of Paul's five years of achievement—the moment for which every young man dreams. Millions of dollars were suddenly dangled before his eyes—incentive for an agreement he was to bitterly regret hardly more than a year later.

Although Paul needed money only for his motion picture projects, unfortunately TV and stage productions were included in an overall agreement that was to place him almost entirely at Goldman's disposal. But past productions were considered a fait accompli and were specifically exempted from the agreement, which became crystallized into a legal entity known as Gregory–Goldman Enterprises, Inc., registered to do business in California and New York as well as in Pennsylvania, headquarters of the Goldman theater chain.

Providing the principals remained on friendly terms and had a mutual understanding, the association could have worked out; but, for all practical purposes, the mechanics of the setup were unworkable. For one thing, the company had six directors, of whom Goldman named two and Gregory two. The latter were lawyer Gordon Youngman and Dorothy Olney, who functioned also as assistant treasurer. In the event of an impasse, it was explained that the company could be dissolved; but this turned out to be far easier said than done.

In addition to *The Naked and the Dead*, other properties acquired for movie production included *The Witch of Guadalupe* and three novels by Thomas Wolfe. The cost of these, plus the investment in the script of Norman Mailer's best-selling book, came to $451,000. It required Charles Laughton a period of nearly eight months and the concentrated efforts of writers Dennis and Terry Saunders, plus several secretaries, to adapt Mailer's script.

Laughton was quoted around Hollywood as having declared that he "hated the assignment." This admission in time reached Goldman, who had not long before played *The Night of the Hunter* in one of his Philadelphia theaters. And Philadelphia chanced to be one of the few important cities in which the picture was badly received. Although he did not have script approval under the agreement with Gregory, Goldman demanded to see the script. Goldman gave it to a director friend in Hollywood to read, and his report was not encouraging. Altogether, this was enough for Goldman, who stopped the flow of funds. Henceforth, Goldman was to devote himself to recouping the $451,000, and Gregory was finally obliged to find a way to repay this sum if he was to have any hope of extricating himself so as to be enabled to proceed with his producing career.

At the same time, Gregory was successfully fulfilling his commitment to CBS television to produce three of the monthly Ford Star Jubilee programs. The first of these, "Three for Tonight," was already a success. The next was an adaptation of *The Caine Mutiny Court Martial*, which was subsequently to be heralded as the dramatic event of the year on TV. Four days before the date of this program, Goldman wired the Hollywood office, demanding credit as joint producer, although he had never made a point of this with the previous TV presentation. Both properties had been specifically exempted, along with other prior productions, from his agreement with Gregory.

Gregory could not at this time have known what was going

on in Goldman's mind. What Paul had not known previous to the association but could have readily ascertained for himself was that Goldman had a facility for litigation. In fact, as the multimillionaire owner of a chain of theaters explained, "He is known to us as an exhibitor who litigated his way into the theater business."

Two days prior to the "Caine Mutiny Court Martial" telecast, Goldman tied up the proceeds from CBS in the New York courts so that no money could be paid out. Salary and other costs of the show added up to a total of very nearly two hundred thousand dollars. This was to prove embarrassing, indeed, in spite of the fact that the producer had delivered admittedly the year's outstanding dramatic program that reaped an unusually high trade rating.

Paul was now in trouble up to his ears—powerless to sign his name or make a move without legal counsel. His attorney, Loyd Wright, secured counsel in New York that got enough of the "Caine Mutiny Court Martial" proceeds freed to pay salaries and most of the other costs. A declaratory and other actions were filed, but motions and appeals take months and then more months to be heard and then finally decided.

In the meantime, two projected stage shows were being held in suspense, and the movie was on the shelf, along with other projected productions. Paul, however, was committed to one more of the monthly Ford Jubilee telecasts over CBS to be done in February 1956. This program he tried to get canceled, and then postponed, but he was held to his contract and forced to produce once more while still in a bind with Goldman. On February 11, he delivered the third notable "spectacular"—"The Day Lincoln Was Shot," the proceeds from which were immediately impounded by the Goldman lawyers.

This time Paul's New York attorneys succeeded only in freeing sufficient funds to defray part of the expenses. There was still another thirty thousand dollars needed to pay the fees of Lillian Gish and Raymond Massey. Once again the former came to the producer's assistance and volunteered to wait until matters were ironed out.

After a brief time, however, Massey's manager threatened suit. This problem was finally resolved through CBS, who generously advanced the producer money with which he could pay this twenty-one-thousand-dollar fee and so avoid still more litigation.

Paul Gregory never received remuneration for delivering the three television programs—all within the period of a year. And, in the meantime, he was continuing to receive overtures from motion picture studios. He had offers up to twenty-five hundred dollars a week (without Laughton) plus a percentage interest for his services as a movie producer only. In addition, he had a similar potential for his services in creating and producing for the stage and TV.

To be sure, Paul had handled himself badly. His arrogance at times alienated those who would have continued to be his friends and whose interest and help at this point would have been invaluable. There were many decisions on which he took no counsel, even from his immediate associates. He always believed in his own self-sufficiency.

Under the terms of a settlement to come, Paul Gregory was bound to repay personally the $451,000 invested by William Goldman in Gregory–Goldman Enterprises, Inc., an investment which he never sought in the first place. Worst of all, the way had now been paved for the break with Charles Laughton.

If the last scene in the mounting spiral of litigation just described could be said to comprise the main act following the Russell Birdwell curtain raiser, unfortunately it was still only laying the groundwork for the climax to come. Charles Laughton was next in line to break with his partner and associate. No one could possibly have contrived a more intricate entanglement—a maze compounded of bad faith, tortuous legalities, and human passion.

Paul, usually a doer and fretful of delays, did not always proceed according to the rule book. And, the more red tape to be unwound, the more he had been all for cutting the corners. It is not possible, or pertinent, here to trace out the maze of developments resulting in the involvement that finally came to a head in June 1956.

During this interim period I revived the dormant Dorian Attractions, Inc., and so continued my booking activities with a few selected independent attractions. Dorothy devoted herself to aiding Paul's efforts to extricate himself. She had supervised the office procedure for some time and was more familiar with the figures than anyone else. One of her best moves previously had been to engage a reliable firm of outside accountants to reorganize and direct the accounting department.

Actually, the Gregory Associates, Inc., company had been doing very well on its stage policy and more than fulfilling expectations. But Paul made the serious error of not taking Loyd Wright's office entirely into his confidence when the association was formed with William Goldman. This was especially important in view of his employment contract with his own company. In the Goldman deal, because Gordon Youngman acted as intermediary in negotiations, he was naturally the attorney to carry through consummation of this arrangement.

But when the Goldman association blew up, it was the Wright office that was called on to help Gregory Associates, Inc., out of its ensuing difficulties. At this critical juncture Laughton was of no help at all; he never rose to the occasion in time of crises in the business department.

It was at this point that lawyer Youngman and agent Robert Coryell were next called on in a further effort to resolve matters. They eventually negotiated a producing deal with RKO Pictures whereby it became possible to effect a settlement with Goldman. RKO agreed not only to take over *The Naked and the Dead* but to make a multimillion-dollar deal with Paul Gregory wherein he was to produce five pictures in three years.

To make the new pact with Goldman firm, however, the signature of Gregory Associates, Inc., was required. Although Paul claimed to have been promised control of his own company so that he would have more freedom of action, it had never been formally given. Loyd Wright then called a special meeting of Gregory Associates, Inc., for June 13 and specified the matters to be brought up. To bypass the unhappy details, the upshot of the meeting was agreement to dissolve Gregory Associates, Inc. As intermediary, Dorothy was appointed to the board for the period of liquidation—somewhat of an anomaly, for she was already a director of Gregory–Goldman Enterprises, Inc.

Even though Paul had retained a sentimental feeling about his company, the action came as a considerable relief. In the beginning of the association Laughton himself was doubtless a dominant influence. But, as Paul gained assurance, he acted more and more independently. It was not in the nature of things that he should ever be given credit for building a second career for Laughton—rebuilding his financial situation at the same time. Thus it was that a highly significant and fruitful partnership in show business was terminated.

An epilogue to the Laughton–Gregory association was to be performed unexpectedly to the accompaniment of crashing glass. Paul came storming into his office one quiet morning. On his seeing Laughton's picture (an original Hirshfield drawing), off came a shoe. Within seconds it landed in the direct center of this once-cherished likeness of his erstwhile associate. A tinkling shower of glass rained to the floor, but the picture itself was undamaged.

It was in the Los Angeles *Times* of June 20, 1956, immediately after the dissolution, that Hedda Hopper wrote, "I saw it coming—the split between Charles Laughton and Paul Gregory—and always thought it was Laughton's talent that put the team over. We'll see how far Gregory gets on his own."

24

End of an *Association*

> "Be satisfied with the
> present and hope for the
> future, profit by the past,
> but don't dwell on it."
> —De Wolf Hopper (at age 77)

In the interim, while litigation was having its day in court, I had taken on the booking of shows for other producers. One of these was the Fujiwara Opera Company of Japan. This was an interesting and colorful company of young Japanese who were schooled in opera of the Western world by Yoshi Fujiwara. Fujiwara was a tenor who had received his training and experience in the opera houses of Italy.

For the American tour, the company was up in two operas— Puccini's *Madame Butterfly* and Gilbert's and Sullivan's *The Mikado*. The former was most delightful and was well received. But the latter was something else. Not only was the company not up to Gilbert and Sullivan, but the conductor was even worse. Furthermore, the management that imported the troupe was completely inept, so the results were somewhat more than the usual headaches for me as tour manager.

Anyway, the tour was completed and the company shipped home three months after arrival.

With Laughton out of the way and his legal troubles in abeyance, Paul Gregory could not wait to get out his next stage production. It was at this point that the incredible happened. He bought the *Billy Barnes Revue*.

This show was not suited for concert-type touring, nor was it a fit successor to its four predecessors. In any event, Charles Laughton was no longer on hand to oppose, and I was never consulted. The decision was Paul's own. The *Billy Barnes Revue* had been running for many weeks in an off-Hollywood setting and was the vehicle whereby young talent showed off some promising new material—satire, music, and sketches. To this rough diamond Paul proceeded to apply the Gregory touch, which was to polish it off for the customers.

He renamed the piece *Foolin' Ourselves*, surely a prophetic title. Then he gave carte blanche to Gene Nelson, a dancer, to stage and rehearse the show. The idea evidently was to elevate a team in the sandlot league to the big time. In some mysterious manner the sparks of genius would somehow ignite and cause it all to blaze. But it never came off.

In the meantime, I had sold a national twelve-week guaranteed tour packed solid with one-night stands. I had assumed that another Gregory success was in the offing without having checked out the preliminaries. But this time the material was not there for a major attraction, and, worse, the show lacked a director who might have made the most out of what there was. But by this time Paul's name had attained a luster nationally, so sponsors also accepted the attraction on faith.

On seeing the first performance when the tour opened, I could scarcely believe the evidence. Paul must have been awaiting confirmation of his own worst fears for, when I called him the next morning and announced the tour must be abandoned, there was no argument against doing so. The leading lady must have been disgusted also; she unexpectedly "became ill," and the tour was canceled.

Not one to take on a situation, it fell to my sad lot to unbook my tour for the producer. Only one who is conscientious and feels deeply the responsibility to local sponsors can appreciate all the implications. And, of course, no one gets paid; and the producer wrote off a $59,000 loss he could ill-afford at this juncture. Unfortunately, I had raised a substantial part of this financing. It might be added here that the *Billy Barnes Revue* reverted to its original habitat in its original form and played for several months.

In the meantime, Paul had acquired another property much more in line with his previous achievements. This was *The Rivalry*, by Norman Corwin. He and Dorothy first saw it in the Circle Theater, and there was no hesitation about wanting it. The piece was promptly contracted, and work started on casting. So, on the demise of *Foolin' Ourselves*, I was able immediately to turn to booking a tour for this reactivated version of the famed Lincoln–Douglas debates.

Corwin also acted as stage director. The device he used to add more human interest was the inclusion of Mrs. Douglas at the debates and on the tour with her husband. The cast consisted of Raymond Massey in his familiar role of Lincoln; Martin Gabel as his political rival, Stephen A. Douglas; and Agnes Moorehead as Mrs. Douglas.

Many reviews pointed out the timeliness of the segregation subject. And the remarkable verbiage, taken directly from the stenographic notes of the times, seemed to apply to some of the

Scene from a Lincoln-Douglas debate as seen by artist Don Freeman a hundred years later.

present problems. Though there was no scenery, the handsome period costumes designed by Walter Plunkett made an appealing stage picture.

Interest in *The Rivalry* tour was augmented by the fact that these historical verbal exchanges anticipated their centennial by only a year.

Having a weakness for Bernard Shaw, I was next attracted to a condensed version of *Back to Methuselah*. The four-hour playing time had been ingeniously shortened to one-half its original length by Arnold Moss. After much overseas correspondence, agreement of the Shaw Estate was eventually forthcoming. I first brought the property to Paul's attention. After giving it some consideration, then going to a tryout performance at a summer playhouse, he turned it down. The property was then taken to Lawrence Langer, head of the Theater Guild. Having eyed the Gregory operation for some time, Langer already had become intrigued with the policy. So he saw his opportunity and immediately called me to make a tour for it.

This one jelled very quickly, although there were bad moments, as usual. Within a week Tyrone Power had been secured, then Faye Emerson was signed as co-star. With Arthur Treacher and Valerie Bettis, the combination of talent was to prove irresistible to the customers.

In the meantime, I proceeded to initiate interest in bookings with a batch of telegrams. After getting the go-ahead in late September, it took seven weeks to shape up an eleven-week tour to begin in January 1958. The casting was well along and the tour almost set before a director was finally secured. Suitable directors in this country were either committed or did not go for the assignment. Finally, it became necessary to look to England for a stage director. At the last minute, Margaret Webster was secured.

The result did not accord with my idea of stylized staging for a concert-type tour. The director had other ideas. The show was built much too heavy for one-night play dates, and about one-third of the physical production was left behind in Florida, where the tour originated.

The attraction quickly picked up momentum and was not

long in garnering weekly grosses up to fifty thousand dollars. It was fortunate for this production that it was moving into a new town almost daily. Although they were able to view an almost unparalleled array of talent on the same stage at the same time, the customers were puzzled to figure out Shaw's meaning. And when the play finally came to rest in New York City, after a record-breaking tour, the customers finally gave up trying to find out and so stayed away.

Back To Methuselah came in to New York with its production costs liquidated and a $78,000 profit in the till—one of the largest out-of-town profits in the forty-year history of the Theater Guild. Unfortunately, this was soon dissipated, and the show closed after running only four weeks.

In the early part of 1958, a script by Leslie Stevens entitled *Man and Woman* was submitted. Both Paul and Dorothy agreed that it was commercial but should be produced only as a conventional theater piece. It was immediately acquired, and a glittering company was secured that represented a return to Gregory's casting efforts at their best. So I arranged a short cross-country tour headed for the bright lights of Broadway. And Dorothy went to work on lining up theater parties, as usual.

Rechristened by Paul *The Marriage-Go-Round*, this one was a commercial piece all about sex and then more sex. It would not have lasted the time of day, however, except that its principal allure was the talents of Claudette Colbert and Charles Boyer. The show continued to be a best-seller on Broadway for over a year and lined its stars' pockets with gold in the meantime. Both were not only paid top salaries, but were also the principal investors.

It was Paul's cancellation of a firm Denver booking for this show that terminated his relations with us. Not always one to adhere to a contract he found too inconvenient or causing an unexpected hardship, Paul canceled this engagement during a period when we were traveling out of the country. He neither asked consultation of any kind nor reimbursed the sponsor, though he promised another show later on.

The cancellation of the en route bookings I had made added up to a total of thirteen weeks of cancellations incidental to four tours. It was my feeling that most of these could have been avoided. Having been in the local management end of the presentations business for so many years, I was always sensitive to the hardships and embarrassments that accompany canceled performances.

I was through covering up and making excuses and wrote Paul Gregory that "cancellations are hard to digest and can ruin one's appetite or even sleep. Certainly they work a genuine hardship on my relations with local managements. . . , and no amount of money can compensate for what it takes out of me. . . . I suggest that we hereafter discontinue our booking arrangement." A quick acceptance was received by return mail.

Having lost Charles Laughton, whose command of stagecraft had made Gregory Associates, Inc., a formidable new force in theater presentation, Gregory had now lost the Olneys, business associates who had contributed a large share to his successes.

Nevertheless, the Laughton–Gregory collaboration had produced a stunning innovation in the style of dramatic presentations—a partnership that will ever retain an important place in the annals of the theater. Among the notable performers who had been presented were Charles Boyer, Sir Cedric Hardwicke, Judith Anderson, Marge and Gower Champion, Harry Belafonte, Henry Fonda, John Hodiak, Raymond Massey, Agnes Moorehead, Lloyd Nolan, and Tyrone Power.

25

Continuation of a Unique Policy

> "The most important thing
> is to have a jolly good
> evening at the theatre.
> And secondly, in the teeth
> of all the evidence, to know
> that life is worth living."
> —Robert Bolt

Neither Charles Laughton nor Paul Gregory ever entirely appreciated or fully understood the implications of the unique policy on which they had accidentally stumbled when *Don Juan in Hell* was launched. In a brief five years it had built to a handsome seven-figure annual gross income and a position of considerable prestige in the presentations business.

It was Dorothy's and my hope that liquidation of Gregory Associates, Inc., would not result in the lapse of such an innovative policy. The idea, however, of stage shows traveling on one-night stands was almost as old as the theater itself—certainly as old as the strolling players of the Middle Ages. In more recent times it took form in the so-called "bus and truck" tours. Just who originated them is not entirely clear, but Sol Hurok certainly had used them effectively for some of his concert and ballet troupes.

The first large-scale proposal to apply this same principle to dramatic shows which was already prevalent in the concert

198

field, was put forth in 1937 by the late Arthur Oberfelder of Denver. He was the dominant concert and show manager of the Rocky Mountain area for a generation. Eminently successful, he conceived the idea of sending out four legitimate shows of Broadway caliber in a season to be sold to local sponsors as a series. They, in turn, would sell tickets for them to their local clienteles on a subscription basis.

Oberfelder mailed an elaborate brochure to prospective sponsors in cities throughout the country. It was the most pretentious piece of selling literature within memory and brought in three hundred thousand dollars' worth of orders. Too late, however, it was found that they could not obtain performance rights to some of the properties concerned. So the project never materialized—at least that was the reason advanced by Fortune Gallo, who was associated with Oberfelder in the venture.

The basic idea, however, was sound. I had always felt sure it would eventuate someday. I never forgot Oberfelder's impressive brochure and kept it in my desk as a reminder. So, when Paul Gregory came along with *Don Juan in Hell* twelve years later, I was quick to grasp at the attraction as the forerunner of a new policy that I felt the country would accept. I envisioned a sort of evolution whereby the concert-type principle of presentation would be applied to dramatic attractions. The result was a stylized, specially devised type of production based on the spoken word.

About the time that the "Hell" show came into being, Dorothy and I had made a ten thousand-mile tour around the country, surveying conditions. Interviewing us upon our return to New York City, *Variety* declared,

> The concert-buying public wants a change . . . . Interest in solo recital attractions is less than ever with group attractions the draw . . . . The Olneys believe that local managers generally will be changing the type of their events more completely than ever in another year—especially if they are deficit shy . . . . They concluded that the so-called "special attractions" of yesterday will become the staple, or subscription, attractions of tomorrow.

Not eager to return to the ranks of producers but eager to

continue the policy, we now had to find either the attractions for touring or another producer to create them. For 1959–1960, the first season entirely on our own, we did both.

Having been approached by Steven Papich, producer of the stage spectacles for the Hollywood Bowl, we took on as our first project its *Gay '90s Night* show. It had grossed over thirty-one thousand dollars in the summer of 1957 (one night) and fifty-three thousand dollars the next season in two nights. So, what could be more logical than that this entertaining spectacle should carry the name of the Hollywood Bowl across the country? It would further add to the fame and prestige of that institution and give it national advertising.

Furthermore, the attraction was almost ready to travel anyway. To create such a production could easily cost $150,000, whereas it would cost only a small fraction of that sum to get this show on the road. By December 1958 the Bowl authorities were convinced. So, the executive committee of the board met under the chairmanship of Z. Wayne Griffin and voted the project.

I was next given the green light to go ahead and arrange the tour. But there was trouble ahead when dissension appeared among the directors of the Hollywood Bowl. Sometime previously, when the fortunes of the Bowl were at an all-time low, Wynn Racamora was brought in as artistic director, and he devised a format for its program that proved eminently successful. In fact, during his five-year tenure, the gross receipts reached record proportions. When asked for his professional advice, Rocamora had also favored the tour. He automatically became the artistic director for the touring production of *Gay '90s Night*, which starred Patricia Morrison.

In the meantime, arrangements for the tour were progressing, and contracts were accumulating for signature. But for the loyalty of Z. Wayne Griffin to the principle of the project, it would have been aborted. The tour had had a great potential and artistically was a genuine credit to the producer, but it never realized its possibilities. It should have become an annual event.

200

The critics were full of enthusiasm. The Charleston *Daily Mail* described it as

> sure to please all comers. And unless you're an ultra-sophisticate who has not a flicker of romance, not a spark of sentimentality, not a trace of nostalgia, you'll kindle a bonfire of enthusiasm as *Gay '90s Night* puts you on the beat and in the groove with tunes which set the toes a-tapping and prove that even in the Gay '90s they had a rock-'n-roll jump in their bustles. Featuring Miss Patricia Morrison in the extraordinary musical extravaganza numbers of the show, the entertainment is really three shows in one — a medley of scenes of yesteryear with the hit tunes of that day; a delightful cream-skimming of the operetta *The Merry Widow*; and showboat time with the era of the minstrel show—a fast-paced, brilliantly costumed, excellently lighted musical show which cannot fail to please every taste.

The national tour drew many enthusiastic and laudatory press notices, although it resulted in a financial loss. The Bowl, however, could well afford to charge this up to national advertising.

The World of Carl Sandburg, written and directed by Norman Corwin, was the other touring vehicle handled by Dorothy and me during the 1959–1960 season. This one was strictly in the Laughton–Gregory tradition, and it achieved a considerable reputation on tour across the country as well as gross receipts in the near vicinity of seven hundred thousand dollars.

For the record, it may be worthwhile here to trace the development of an important stage attraction from its inception. This one resulted from a program presented at the University of California in Los Angeles titled *A Tribute to Carl Sandburg*. For thirty years a student of the celebrated poet and author, Norman Corwin was named to make the selections from his works and to write the necessary continuity. Hollywood celebrities read the various Sandburg items, and the resulting program was eminently successful.

Conforming the material from the Sandburg program into a stage presentation for touring on the road was not so easy. But Corwin accomplished the impossible in brilliant fashion.

Through a publicist, Judd Bernard, we met Armand Deutsch, financier and movie producer. Fascinated with the project, he was not long in agreeing to become producer, and he wrote the check for $81,000 that launched the enterprise.

The project did not finally jell until May, so getting this tour launched while cleaning up the *Gay '90s Night* tour occupied my summer. The ever-efficient Dorothy became general manager for the Sandburg show. The matter of securing a big-name star was solved by Judd Bernard, who was instrumental in securing Bette Davis and her husband, Gary Merrill, as co-star. This was a real bit of offbeat casting. Bette accepted the rigors of touring with fairly good grace. But she was restless, seldom happy, always shifting hotel reservations, and at times seemed to live in a state bordering on turmoil.

As the tour progressed, however, and the company became seasoned, business improved as well as the size of the audiences. Receipts in Chicago (where the show set a house record of $41,000 in a week at the Civic Theater) and in Los Angeles ($124,000 after taxes in four weeks) were particularly impressive. Also, Bette received and enjoyed a personal acclaim that was heartwarming to this accomplished performer. Gary Merrill also received enthusiastic press notices, as did Barry Sullivan, who replaced him for five weeks because of a film commitment.

To Armand Deutsch goes the credit for developing a distinguished attraction. He did not stint but did everything within his power to make the show a success and to keep the star in good spirits. The latter task, however, proved to be difficult. But she was superb in her assignment.

Finally, to the stature of Carl Sandburg's already monumental achievements as a writer was added acclaim for his first stage piece. He was fortunate in having such an able partisan in Norman Corwin. For, like Stephen Vincent Benét's *John Brown's Body*, the poems were neither intended nor written for stage presentation. Fortunate it is that such literature could be so successfully adapted and its wealth of ideas thereby vastly extended.

Hedda Hopper wrote that "Bette Davis can outact anyone!" The cast and author-adapter Corwin received merited acclaim;

but the words of Sandburg drew the deepest appreciation. "Sandburg's words are so pungent and vivid in their expression that, of themselves, they vibrate with the excitement we call theater" was the opinion of the *Hartford Courant*. And the *Boston Globe* said, "The sort of words actors like to speak and the public likes to hear spoken."

The World of Carl Sandburg added up to a total of seven concert-type dramatic attractions that Dorothy and I had managed and booked for national tours. All were especially created and produced for the purpose primarily of national touring; and all but one showed a profit, usually substantial. Of these seven, we were responsible for guiding four onto Broadway, all of which were successful artistically as well as financially.

A new mode of stage presentation that was begun almost by accident had by now demonstrated its worth. Imitators were many but, with one or two exceptions, did not make the big time. The formula seemed simple, but it was also complex and beset with pitfalls. With our perspective and experience we had become its most successful protagonists. And so we continued to work wholeheartedly to insure continuity of the policy.

26

Great Castles of Britain

"Many a tower which, when
it frowned
With all its battlements,
was only terrible,
Time has mouldered into
beauty."
—Anonymous

In the interval between shifting our base of operations from the West Coast back to New York, Dorothy and I decided to avail ourselves of the opportunity to make a documentary film featuring some of the old castles of England and Scotland.

On previous visits we had been intrigued by the many-storied romance that still clung to these fascinating reminders of medieval times "when knighthood was in flower." As the idea took root and blossomed, the day of decision finally arrived. We found ourselves committed to an exciting adventure that overrode the many problems as well as the roadblocks that interposed themselves along the way.

Initially, the thought of contriving a presentation that could be contained in a can and shown at will had an enormous appeal. We would be thereby bypassing performers and their temperaments, agents and their deviousness, unions and their extravagant demands, and all the rest of the trappings that conspire to make stage attractions in these times more a hardship than a pleasure to handle. But, actually, it was not that simple, as we shall see. Anyway, this was to be a creative activity that we originated and carried out from idea to can. For better or worse, we were to gain pleasure and satisfaction, as well as abundant experience, from the doing.

We were to be encouraged and abetted in our efforts by James McLeod, British consul in Los Angeles, and Dame Flora McLeod (no apparent relation). The latter, well into her seventies, was the only woman head of a Scottish clan. We were fortunate in meeting her during the course of a world tour on which she was raising money from McLeods, here and there, for the preservation of ancient Dunvegan Castle on the Isle of Skye—home base of the McLeod clan.

No one knows how many medieval castles once existed in Britain. Dorothy's extended research over two years seemed to indicate, however, that there were around one thousand of them still scattered along the seacoasts and in other strategic locations. She researched the stories of seven hundred castles, choosing seventy-two when we finally got to laying out the itinerary. Fortunately, the Huntington Library in Pasadena made available from its archives important source material that was of immense help in the preparation. This material included the Annals of the House of Percy which had been deposited in the library's vaults.

Letters then went out to officials as well as to owners and managers of the seventy-two castles. The National Trust made available its properties and notified its custodians in advance of our coming. Cooperation all along the way was splendid. A fixed route was set up, to which we strictly adhered, for the British are meticulous on dates and appointments. In most localities we made a point of staying at old inns—not always modern in conveniences but usually replete with good food and atmosphere.

When we arrived in London our first problem was to secure possession of our film. By air cargo we had shipped ahead one hundred reels of Kodachrome 16mm. film, which we found was being held at the Victoria Docks subject to import duties and sales taxes amounting to several hundred dollars. At a previous meeting in Los Angeles, a member of Parliament had become interested in our project and offered to help when we arrived in London. He was promptly contacted, and the next day our carton of film was mysteriously delivered to our room in Brown's Hotel.

Another unforeseen snag developed when we discovered that electrical outlets and their fittings in different cities were of varying specifications. There were two prongs and three prongs; some prongs were spaced differently; others were round and some flat, etc. To meet this contingency we stopped at a Woolworth's in Harrogate and bought a sample of each plug, then had them wired up in combinations so that our equipment could function under any conditions. We also procured a converter whereby our tape recorder could be activated from the battery of our car.

After meetings with officials at the Foreign Office, the National Trust, and the British Travel Association, we were off to our first castle in Colchester. Actually, most of the ancient keep, the walls, and other appurtances had long since disappeared. About all that remained was some of the foundation, which had been roofed to serve as a museum. Once a Saxon stronghold, under the Romans Colchester had become the most important city in all of Britain.

It is not feasible to recount here our day-to-day experiences as we moved from castle to castle. All we can do is to highlight some of the more important castles and their characteristics. From Colchester we proceeded north, stopping next at the historic Shakespeare Inn in Stratford-on-Avon.

In the near vicinity we were able to film Broughton Castle in famed Banbury; Warwick Castle, perfectly preserved as a museum and a residence for the earl; and Kenilworth Castle, its imposing ruins reminiscent of those days of glory when Leicester feted Queen Elizabeth with a magnificent pageant on his private lake.

We came next to picturesque Rockingham Castle, situated on a height overlooking the Welland Valley. Built by William the Conqueror, it served for five centuries as the favorite hunting lodge for the kings of England.

At Raby Castle, Lord Barnard maintains a private deer park, in the center of which is the finest inhabited fortress in the north of England. Its medieval kitchen, perfectly preserved, was of special interest. Not so long ago it required a staff of thirty-eight to maintain the ninty-nine rooms; today most of the rooms are closed off, and the staff is reduced to three.

Until it was demolished by gunfire, Bamborough Castle dominated the North Sea coast, which it was designed to protect. Fortunately for this generation, it has been restored by its owner, Lord Armstrong.

Next we approached the striking ruins of Warkworth Castle on its strategic height above the rippling Coquet River. Here was the seat of the powerful Percys, whose business was fighting and intrigue. The third Percy and his son, Harry Hotspur, were renowned warriors. After being instrumental in placing Henry IV on the throne later they hatched the conspiracy against the same king in the very rooms we filmed. It was in these rooms that three of the scenes from Shakespeare's *Henry IV* are laid.

Proceeding on the great North Road to Scotland, we passed through the ancient gateway as we approached the dark, menacing barbican of Alnwick Castle. Inside, the visitor first approaches the Auditor's Tower, where the sixth earl imprisoned his auditor until he could account for more money received than he had previously turned over. The entire fabric has been well-preserved and constitutes one of the finest examples of medieval military architecture.

Hoghton Tower gave us another exciting experience, also replete with dramatic stories of adventure and romance. It was in August 1617, that Sir Richard Hoghton was host to a visit by King James I and his retinue. For the occasion the long ascent to the tower was carpeted along its entire length with red velvet. Sir Cuthbert told us at luncheon that, according to the records, his family spent two generations paying for the carpet and the party given for His Majesty. Legend maintains that the beef served so pleased the king that he drew his sword and knighted the steak Sir Loin.

When we entered Scotland, our first contact was at Lennoxlove House in East Lothian. Formerly known as Lethington Castle, it is the residence of the Duke of Hamilton—a most interesting example of the transition of a castle into a house. Relics of the martyred Mary, Queen of Scots, are on view as well as the map carried by the Nazi Rudolph Hess when he landed on the duke's estate during World War II.

Highlight of the tour in the north was, indeed, Edinburgh Castle, where the Ministry of Works had made preparation for our reception. We were privileged to film for the first time the "Honors of Scotland"—the Crown Jewels (lost for 109 years); the tiny room in which Mary gave birth to James VI in 1566; Queen Margaret's chapel; and other historic treasures. The history of Scotland is mirrored in this ancient fortress—a dark, brooding history of intrigue, murder, and battle adorned by bravery.

Other castles filmed in this area were Craigmillar, Stirling, and Glamis. The latter is probably the most legendary, as well as the most haunted, of the Scottish castles. Many stirring events occurred within its walls, including the murder of King Duncan by Macbeth and, in recent times, the birth of the Queen Mother Elizabeth.

One of the best-preserved and maintained of the privately owned castles is Blair Atholl, dating from the thirteenth century. The duke had on hand for our arrival his personal pipers, who recorded for us a traditional wedding march.

From Inverness we proceeded south through the Great Glen that sunders the Highlands and contains in its mighty chasm Loch Ness, famous today as the reputed home of Nessie the monster. Before leaving the picturesque Loch we were intrigued by the ruins of Urquhart Castle, a victim of clan warfare and finally pillaged by the local gentry. Today they could well remind us of "the gaunt, ghostly, and ghastly" edifices once described by Bobby Burns.

From Drumnadrochit our route took us through the Highlands, then by ferry to our next destination. Dunvegan Castle on the misty Isle of Skye is steeped in fairy legend and most famous of the Hebridean strongholds. Here we were entertained by Dame Flora McLeod, who had invited us as her guests sometime earlier in Los Angeles. At an evening gathering we were privileged to record the story of the "Fairy Flag" as narrated by Dame Flora herself. Then we were invited to a homely frolic in the village hall, where we recorded a *Ceilidh*, the Gaelic term for an informal concert. It was only reluctantly that we departed Skye to fulfill a domineering schedule.

The ancestral home of the duke of Argyll is Inverary Castle, well preserved and loaded with treasures inside. Then followed in succession Carrickfergus and Dunluce castles in northern Ireland; and Craignethan, Caerlaverock, and Sizergh in England—all reeking with history and tempting to the photographer.

In Wales we first visited Chirk Castle near Wrexham, a typical border fortress of the time of Edward II. Lt. Col. Ririd Myddleton and his lovely wife were charming hosts, and we were regaled with stories of his ancestors, one of whom had sailed the seven seas with Sir Walter Raleigh and had thereby acquired the means to purchase this property in 1595.

Next on the list was Conway Castle, one of the most elaborate castellated establishments dating from the era beginning with Edward I. It was not long after this period that castle building (fortified dwellings of the noble gentry) ceased. Dynamite and cannon fire, as practiced by Oliver Cromwell and his Roundheads, were their doom.

From its craggy summit, Conway Castle dominated a medieval town—the only community in Britain still embraced within its almost intact walls. This was our forty-second castle—each one different and more interesting than the last. Conway represented castle building at its peak. It was a vast fabric containing eight turrets, and there were twenty-one towers and five gateways inserted into the walls at regular intervals. Unfortunately, space is too limited here to enlarge on all the ramifications of this grand structure.

After a brief interlude of relaxation in Llandudno on the north coast, we drove on to Beaumaris Castle, a more modest structure but retaining all the appurtenances of a typical early Edwardian fortress—moat, portcullis, barbican, and curtain walls sixteen feet thick.

After driving thirty miles along the Menai Straits, we arrived at the greatest of the castles built by King Edward I: Caernarvon. Approached from across the Seiont River, it was, indeed, a majestic sight. Built on a Roman site, there are still portions of the ancient walls that once surrounded the town. Although assaulted on three different occasions, the castle has come down through the ages almost intact. Caernarvon is celebrated today as the place chosen in 1301 for the investiture of the heir to the British throne as the Prince of Wales.

Located in the heart of Wales, Powis Castle is surrounded by pretentious formal gardens said to be the finest in all Britain. There are four terraces (two hundred yards long) with hanging gardens, clipped yews, conventional statuary, and elaborate balustrades—all surrounded by acres of flowering laburnum and rhododendron. An interesting room in the castle is devoted to relics of Clive of India, father of the third earl of Powis. This castle was never assaulted at any time and is now a property of the National Trust.

Of the thirty-two castles on the Welsh border, Ludlow was the most important. Unfortunately, it is still in private hands, and the condition of its ruins was deplorable. Here it was in 1633 that Milton's *Masque of Comus* was written and first produced. A modern production was in preparation on the day of our visit.

The most memorable feature of the buildings at Sudeley Castle was the perfectly preserved Norman chapel. Buried inside in a marble crypt, beneath a richly colored stained glass window, are the mortal remains of Catherine Parr. She was the only wife of King Henry VIII, who was able to enjoy the martyrdom of being his widow.

Berkeley Castle stands out as the most complete and well-operated castle in our experience, We were hosted by Captain Berkeley, a direct descendant of the family that has continuously occupied this noble property for over eight hundred years. Among his ancestors was Sir William Berkeley, who became governor of Virginia in 1641. One of the historical features is the guardroom in which King Edward II was murdered and the breach in one of the walls made by Cromwell's cannon. Maintained in sumptuous quarters with four full-time keepers was a pack of seventy-eight foxhounds—one of the three oldest packs in continuous existence in the kingdom. These were put on special display for the benefit of my camera.

Ever since 1404 the Luttrell family have been lords of Dunster Castle, a beautiful property they can no longer afford to own and maintain. Nestling at the base of the tor is the charming old village of Dunster, and on the opposite side is the Exmoor Valley, of Lorna Doone fame.

We arrived at the most legendary ruins of all on the coast of Cornwall: Tintagel Castle. This is the reputed site of the birth of King Arthur (about 450 A.D.)—a spectacular location on a rockbound crag washed by Atlantic waves. A one-time stronghold of the earls of Cornwall, much of the fabric has now slipped into the sea, leaving only ragged traces of its former glory.

No so far distant is Penzance, from which we had to secure a boat in order to film St. Michael's Mount. Surrounded by the sea and strategically located on its timeless base of living rock, the castle was originally begun as a monastery by Edward the Confessor in pre-Norman times. It, too, has a fascinating story and is now a property of the National Trust.

Corfe Castle, on the Sussex Coast, is another sad reminder of the terrible damage wrought by Cromwell and his army as they sought to destroy the strongholds of royalty. Instead of "Lord Protector," he should have gone down in history as the "Destroyer." After withstanding Cromwell's siege for three long years, it had to finally pay the extreme penalty and was ordered demolished. Even in their present state, the grandeur of these ruins is a continual reminder that here formerly stood one of the most formidable castles in all Europe.

For the record, I must call attention to Bodiam, Saltwood, Portchester, Rochester, and Pevensey castles—all unique and surely worth much more than the passing notice given to them here. Pevensey Castle is of particular interest. It was here on the pebbly beach of Pevensey Bay that Claudius Caesar launched the first successful conquest of Britain in 43 A.D. Then, 1023 years later, on the same beach, Duke William of Normandy began the second and last successful invasion of the island. So, inside the original walls and bastions, there are the ruins of the Norman keep—a castle within a castle.

To repel the expected Spanish invasion centuries later, Queen

Elizabeth had cannons installed on the embankment outside the Roman walls. Further precautions were also taken at the time of the threatened Napoleonic invasion. Finally, in our own time, machine gun nests were installed in the ruined towers to forestall the proposed conquest of the island by Hitler.

A short distance farther, along the Channel Coast, we arrived at Dover, with its imposing and famous castle dominating the cliffs behind the town. The fortress is maintained in all its original glory plus later additions. Within the walls are the Chapel of St. Mary (oldest in England) and the Pharos, or lighthouse—the oldest Roman ruin surviving in Britain. It would require another book to relate the fabulous story of Dover Castle, but we must now move on to London and the climax of this journey.

The Tower of London was built by William the Conqueror in 1079 on an old Roman site. It was inhabited by kings of England down through James I. The Tower has served both as a refuge and a prison for several kings and queens. In more recent times, Rudolph Hess was held a prisoner here. And the courtyard has been the scene of many important executions. The towers in the surrounding walls have been witness to much history—sometimes gallant deeds and occasionally dark crimes. The structure has remained almost unaltered throughout nine centuries. Today it serves chiefly as a museum housing a fabulous armory and many other relics of the past.

On our final day we called on the Ministry of Works and the National Trust to pay our heartfelt thanks for their splendid cooperation, without which we would not have dared this undertaking. Altogether we had driven our once-new Jaguar over four thousand miles; lodged at thirty-four ancient hostelries; and filmed seventy-two castles. Of these, forty-four were to remain in the edited film. There were ten thousand feet that had to be refined down to two thousand feet for the purpose of our lectures.

All in all, the summer of 1958 represented a memorable adventure that vastly enhanced our knowledge of, and admiration for, our mother country.

212

27

National Performing Arts, Inc.

"Broadway is a good place
in which to make a fortune,
but no place to earn a living."
—*Brooks Atkinson*

For the second half of our second score of years in the presentations business, we were to move back to the other side of the continent and operate out of New York City. This move was partly the result of a need to be closer to the main source of stage shows for touring and partly the result of an invitation to head up the theater division of the newly formed United Performing Arts, Inc.

This new company was the brainchild of Harlowe Dean, formerly a vice-president of National Concert and Artists Corporation, where he was in charge of its Civic Concerts Service. When this company acquired new ownership, he decided that his nineteen years spent in developing organized audiences for concerts should be put to still better use on a broader scale.

Dean formed United Performing Arts, Inc., to add other cities to those already organized for concert giving and to organize theater subscription series throughout the country. This was a big order that required financing, which he conveniently found in Wall Street (of all places). Everything was gilt-edged—the corporate lawyers were Sullivan and Cromwell; auditors were Price-Waterhouse and Company; and the attorneys for the new enterprise were Paul, Weiss, Rifkind, Wharton, and Garrison, represented by Robert Montgomery.

United Performing Arts was operating for nearly a year prior to my becoming manager and booker for its theater division. In the meantime, an annual overhead in staff and expenses of well into six figures had been committed.

The pilot city that was first to be organized for theater was Toledo. Gradually, other communities were added; but it was uphill going, and contracting shows, with Columbia Artists Management already in this field, was a problem. CAMI, as this firm was known, had been one of two leading agencies in the concert field for thirty years. Thinking to emulate the success of its Community Concert Service in forming organized concert series in hundreds of cities, it decided to apply the same technique to the presentation of Broadway shows. CAMI, however, lacked a theater executive with know-how and was not long in discovering that stage shows and musical concerts are vastly different. An outstanding success in the latter, it came up a cropper with the former.

While CAMI was still licking its wounds, Harlowe Dean, ambitious for his new enterprise, negotiated to buy out the Broadway Theater Alliance from CAMI with the help of $45,000 from his bankers. In less than three years of wooing theatergoers from coast to coast, CAMI had organized theater buffs in eighty-two communities. Within a year United Performing Arts had added another ten cities so that by the season of 1963–1964 it had a bona fide national theater audience of well over 1,200,000 hard-ticket buyers—an achievement from any standpoint.

It was my function to provide the attractions with which to feed this monster. Not only was this task onerous in itself but it was also compounded by Dean's lack of theater experience, which meant delays and difficulties in getting approvals. Then there were other failures of management, which were represented by a total loss exceeding $600,000 in four years.

This led to a discontinuance of the flow of investment monies and eventually to a breakup of United Performing Arts. Dean then took over the concert division; operated it for a few years under the name of United Audience Service, Inc.; and finally it ceased altogether. Then I acquired the theater division, which was renamed National Performing Arts, Inc. In less than a year the annual deficit was reduced from $200,000 to $19,000. But this was hardly good enough.

By the season of 1963–1964 I had seven shows on the road under the aegis of NPA. They were *The Sound of Music, A Man for All Seasons, Mary, Mary, Just Twenty Plus Me, The Boys from Syracuse, A Thousand Clowns,* and *Camelot.* NPA was now grossing an annual rate of five million dollars and still losing money.

On the road there were five trained organizers servicing the Broadway Theater Leagues and costing an average of $14,000 apiece. Altogether, the annual overhead had mounted to $184,000 for a staff of thirteen. I was working ten-hour days six days a week, trying desperately to keep seven touring shows booked into profit and, at the same time, maintaining the Broadway Theater League circuit.

A word here is appropriate about the Broadway Theater Leagues, which were originally organized by the Broadway Theater Alliance under Columbia Artists Management, Inc. The basic concept sounded simple enough: organize a subscription series in a community, then block book four or five shows with the subscription money obtained from a campaign. In other words, a series of shows could presumably be booked as easily as a single performance could be sold separately (according to the theory). But it did not work out that way — simplicity became complexity.

Theater is something very special! It seldom conforms. In professional (or commercial) theater the producers are disorganized. The conditions under which they operate have become much too onerous for any but the very hardy, or the unwary novice. Hence, the prime source of supply for the BTI was wrought with so many uncertainties and so beset with such a multitude of vicissitudes as to make every season a scramble in order to secure those shows that would satisfy the BTL formula. This was based on having a comedy, a drama, a musical, and a fourth show—all of which must be outstanding.

And, of course, the customers expect to have known stars. But, in these days of the great mass media, anyone bearing even a slight resemblance to being a star will not submit to the rigors of modern travel—comfortable as it is compared with conditions at the turn of the century.

At that time, there were reportedly three thousand one- and two-night stands. With the advent of movies and the other mass media, these had shrunk in recent years to a mere handful—twenty-one prime cities that had Theater Guild subscription, and about two dozen so-called intermediate cities. This trend National Performing Arts did more than any other organization to reverse. Eventually, it built the number of road stands back to an aggregate of over three hundred cities and towns in which my shows were booked on one- and two-night stands.

In the Sunday issue of October 11, 1964, John Keating wrote in the *New York Times*,

There is pretty general agreement that a man named Julian Olney is among those most responsible for making the new deal work. "Without him," admits a basically antagonistic competitor, "there would be no bus and truck business."

The road, as generations of actors knew it, had all but disappeared before the start of World War II. The "National Company" of a Broadway hit might play extended stands at ten or fifteen major cities—and that was it. The traditional touring company, with its split weeks and one-night stands, was as close to extinction as burlesque or the small-town fight club.

Railroads, devastated by the competition of the airplane, the automobile and the tractor-trailer truck, were no longer able to handle the true road company. Major roads had closed their offices in many key cities. In others, they were down to one-train-a-day departures. The new streamliners, in many cases the only through service between major cities, weren't carrying baggage cars.

Faced with such a situation, producers had to decide either to quit the road altogether, or find some new way to make the journey. The bus and truck combination was the answer.

Mr. Olney's indispensable contribution was his missionary work among the culturally inclined matrons and businessmen of towns that had not seen live actors for twenty or thirty years. He built up a network of "guaranteed" audiences, arranged sponsorship of bused-in productions by local groups and set up the line of march.

Not being able to control the source of productions to assure availability of the right attractions at the right time was not the only major problem. Organizing new BTLs and reviving the sagging fortunes of the weaker units in the circuit required constant supervision.

When the decision had been made to organize a city, a trained representative was sent out to prepare the groundwork. He would call on leading citizens and educators, housewives, and businessmen and form a group that would organize a nonprofit Broadway Theater League. This operation depended on volunteer help for manpower. The procedure was all laid out in a carefully prepared manual which outlined every step. The main idea was to bring current Broadway productions to smaller communities at no financial risk locally.

Once the sponsoring organization was formed, there was a kickoff dinner. Talks were given, the shows for the first season were described, and the campaign workers were organized and instructed. At one time it was estimated that there were over ten thousand volunteer workers enlisted on behalf of Broadway shows throughout the country. The subscription campaign would usually last a week, sometimes longer if the goal had not been reached. Preliminary expense money (usually around twenty-five hundred dollars) was advanced from New York and later liquidated from the BTL income. Only season subscribers could attend; tickets to single events were not sold, except in the case of subscribers who were bringing guests.

The local BTL contracted with the Broadway Theater Alliance (later on it was to be United Performing Arts, Inc.) for its shows. For its trouble, the parent organization in New York received annually a fee based on the number of subscribers secured.

In general terms, it was figured that the budgets for shows should be $14,500, in addition to which there were the local expenses. A league was not considered "safe" unless it had at least fifteen hundred subscribers. There were a number of leagues that made substantial profits, which had to be given away in order to maintain their tax-free status. The Junior League of Little Rock, Arkansas, for instance, had a goal of fifty thousand dollars, which it eventually contributed to a new arts center. In Tulsa, South Bend, and Utica, substantial sums were contributed annually to local colleges (usually for drama scholarships). The Broadway Theater League in Evansville, Indiana, ran an annual playwriting contest.

During the season of 1963–1964, bus and truck wheels rolled 106,741 miles back and forth through forty states from September to May for National Performing Arts, Inc. They were carrying five shows coast to coast, visiting the one- and two-night stands for the first time with *Camelot*, *A Man for All Seasons*, *The Boys from Syracuse*, and *A Thousand Clowns*. They carried also *The Sound of Music* and *Mary, Mary* to continue their successful tours of the previous season and play for those cities still waiting for them.

A total of 278 actors and staff members rode and sang in those buses, stopped at the hamburger stands along the way, and dined in motels and hotels before going into their performances at theaters and auditoriums. They played in towns and cities varying in population from fifteen thousand to one million.

In the meanwhile, box offices in 171 cities had sold over 1,200,000 tickets, sometimes as far ahead as a year. Of these, 83 were Broadway Theater Leagues and a few other subscription cities. Ticket buyers, who averaged three dollars a ticket for straight shows and four dollars for musicals, paid more than five million dollars over box-office counters, at ticket booths in music and department stores, at various meetings, and by mail.

The 128 weeks played by these stage shows included over 850 live performances. Only five performances in all were canceled—two because of blizzards, and on the night of the Kennedy assassination three of the shows did not play. All but one of these missed performances were subsequently made up.

The old show-biz rule "the show must go on" prevailed and added zest to the entertainment of many communities.

The myriad problems incidental to creating, maintaining, and servicing ninety-two Broadway Theater Leagues were almost beyond comprehension. Local groups sometimes wanted shows outside of those offered; traveling representatives had to be continually on call and so plan their time as to coincide with the local campaigns as they were scheduled; shows often were too slow in being contracted; stars were announced who later on changed their minds and so had to be replaced; the occasional cancellation of a tour would unnerve some of the local groups, who declared this to be a "crazy business," and they wanted no part of it in the future; stagehand demands in some towns were ridiculous and upset many a carefully planned local budget; spacing the play dates of the shows at monthly intervals was always a problem; and so on ad infinitum.

As a result, more than one-half of the original BTL cities gave up. In the course of the shaking-down process, some of these cities would have fallen by the wayside in any event; but many of them could have been maintained. Those that survived had strong local leadership and support that persisted against the process of erosion.

Nevertheless, the basic idea had been good. It had an enormous advantage over some of the big-city subscription series, which each year had to accept some new and untried shows ("prior to Broadway") to fill out their schedules. On the other hand, the BTL cities usually had the pick of the tried-and-true available shows. How else could Waterloo, Iowa, for instance, present *Mary, Mary, Camelot, A Shot in the Dark,* and *The Sound of Music* in a single season? These companies were all Broadway caliber—sometimes even better. The only difference was in the physical production, which had to be lightened owing to the exigencies of road travel.

Probably the biggest drawback to maintainance of such a nationwide Broadway Theater League operation was the inability to control the sources of production. Although the BTLs were bound to National Performing Arts for their source of supply by a "best efforts" contract, the time arrived when some shows had to be obtained from outside sources. NPA would contract certain shows for delivery to its affiliates, but these did not always take all the shows offered.

Then, when outside agencies secured the rights to product required to supply the BTLs, matters became further complicated. The commercial producers could not care less about the continued existence of the BTL circuit, although, in the long run, it would have been in their own best interests to cooperate. The commercial theater is an "every man for himself" business. The League of New York Theaters, which claimed to have some interest in the road, did virtually nothing to sustain the new road operation that was grossing several million dollars annually and was of immense benefit to its members. And some of the touring companies were paying a weekly royalty, originally fifty dollars, and more recently seventy-five dollars, into the league's till. For all of which the new touring circuit received almost nothing; so the half-million dollars spent in creating it was lost, never to be recouped.

By this time it had become only too apparent that the whole BTL operation, useful as it was in reviving the road and bringing professional theater to avid playgoers, was not a job for private enterprise. The obvious answer seemed to be foundation support, which will be dealt with shortly. In the meantime, I had no choice but to slash the staff by over one-half; drop BTLs that were so marginal as to pose a constant threat of loss; and then cut down the number of touring shows to two or three a season. It was not always easy to conform to a policy of touring only first-class theater nationally. And those BTLs that had developed adequate leadership and experience would have to survive on their own. So the continuance of a policy whereby four Broadway shows would be provided annually to the ninety-two BTL cities that had been contracted proved well-nigh impossible. The erosion of the new theater circuit was, indeed, a major disappointment.

The dissemination of Broadway "beyond Broadway" was basically a good idea. For a few years, over three hundred cities were to benefit. The Broadway Theater Leagues had become the largest new class of show sponsors in the country. They extended all the way from Tacoma, Yakima, and Vancouver in the Northwest to Grand Junction and Pueblo in Colorado; to Wichita Falls, Texas; to Topeka, Kansas, and on to the Eastern seaboard. Every section of the country was represented. It had become a vast system that became too unwieldy to support privately.

A final effort to salvage the Broadway Theater League operation was made by formation of the National Performing Arts Foundation, Inc. Theoretically, foundation grants would be awarded on the basis of need and merit. There were, however, political considerations, which will probably never be eliminated or even admitted. The goal whereby first-class touring theater would be available to over a hundred cities, in addition to the usual prime cities, was eminently worthwhile.

Seven leading foundations were approached with a well-devised presentation. They were not impressed, however, and all we received for our trouble were seven turndowns. W. McNeill Lowry (vice-president for the humanities and the arts of the Ford Foundation) regretted the lack of sufficient funds so "that we are not able to give you encouragement about the National Performing Arts Foundation." This was, of course, sidestepping the issue. It was not much later that he reportedly gave a new acting group over $1,000,000. Previously that group had received $500,000. While this company had a worthy objective, it still had to demonstrate its worth. We were asking only for $300,000 to continue a proved operation. Previously, the Ford Foundation was reported to have made grants totaling $232,000,000 on behalf of the performing arts.

Aided and abetted by Willard Espey as consultant, it had required over two years of effort and a final prod from Sen. Jacob Javits to secure tax exemption approval from the Internal Revenue Service for the NPA Foundation. It had a prestigious board, headed by Dr. Ralph Frost of the University of Tennessee, and it had all the machinery set up for realizing its objective—the delivering of professional theater to an established circuit of theaters throughout the nation. Under the circumstances, and lacking further financing, the organization had to be disbanded and the entire project abandoned.

Robert M. Weitman, an independent producer, called the shots when he declared in weekly *Variety* that

> There are no rules of the game. The players who win more than they lose are . . . gamblers. They are sometimes called geniuses, experts, or talents, . . . they are a breed apart.
>
> In any other business, the product can be tested, anticipated, manufactured on an assembly line and placed on the market. In show business the major testing and anticipation of a fickle public comes after the fact, not before. Therefore, the gamble is greater and the high-rollers of show business toss their dice into whirlwinds . . . . There is no business like show business.

Richard Maney (ex-dean of theater press agents) once stated that "legit . . . is the only free agent in the entertainment world. . . . Although it may continue to contract, it will never die . . . can never be replaced or equalled by mechanical gimmicks and gadgetry."

In the meantime, during the brief tenure of the Broadway Theater League circuit, we had delivered on national tour over thirty professional productions. Highlights of these tours are described in the following two chapters.

28

The Play's the Thing: Musicals

> *"Plays and players are 'the brief chronicles of the time,' the epitome of human life and manners."*
> —*William Hazlitt, 1818*

Selecting and contracting plays and musicals for either national touring or Broadway Theater League purposes were no easy tasks. And it is a considerable responsibility. One's own taste is not necessarily in accord with public taste. At the same time, it had been always our aim to present first-class attractions that proved worthwhile entertainment. This principle was adhered to from the outset.

Some productions do not pay their way, especially ballets and symphony orchestras. Hence the value of the well-organized subscription series.

In the early 1960s there was an ample supply of so-called Broadway "product" from which to choose. Hence there was room in which to maneuver. If a certain show presented difficulties, then there were others to be approached. The important thing was to get a good show that would be acceptable to this extended market.

There was, and still is, a segment of the country known as the Bible Belt. It is still too important to be ignored in making up a national tour. In Brownwood, Texas, for instance, the sponsor insisted that the one line of profanity in *Barefoot in the Park* be deleted. And when *Man of La Mancha* arrived in Memphis early in 1969, a considerable stir was aroused by the "abduction" number, also known as the "rape scene." Ordinarily, this dance number would be taken in stride and scarcely gain passing notice. But not in Memphis. The police were called out to stop the show, and letters to the editor were written and published in the local press. Memphis, however, having only recently survived the crisis of desegregating its public facilities, rode out this storm, and the show went on.

Then there are the sophisticates to be satisfied in other areas. Many of the Broadway Theater Leagues were in smaller communities where the patrons wanted, first and foremost, top entertainment with a Broadway label and reviews that would inspire subscription sales.

By this time it was axiomatic that any and every theater series must be headlined by a hot Broadway musical. And if such was not available, then one of lesser stature would be acceptable, but a new musical there must be.

My entrée into the Broadway field was provided by the late Harold Goldberg, executive director of the Independent Booking Office. It was on his recommendations that the door was opened for securing *The Music Man* and *My Fair Lady* for bus and truck touring. The former was the first major Broadway musical show to be conformed and booked on short-term engagements from one-night to split-week stands.

Kermit Bloomgarden was the successful producer of *The Music Man*, which was still playing on Broadway after four years, when it was decided in 1961 to do the bus and truck tour. The Broadway show had twenty scene changes and drew over fifteen hundred amperes of electric current backstage. Obviously, it had to be conformed for my tour. So, I worked with Howard Bay, the show's designer, to devise a "soft" production using traveler curtains and set pieces that could be conveniently stacked in a forty-foot trailer van.

Of necessity, every touring show must deliver a first-rate acting company; otherwise it would not be accepted locally. But physical production has to be cut down somewhat for the one-

and two-night stands. This had been a cardinal virtue of the Charles Laughton shows: a brilliant cast of performers whereas physical production was negligible (to the stagehands' disappointment). As a matter of fact, three of these shows had come off the road tours and been presented on Broadway without the benefit even of a scenic designer's services.

The Music Man company traveled 24,000 miles to play 229 performances in 112 cities in 43 states. Gross receipts aggregated $1,325,000—a record at that time. For the first time, the feasibility of presenting a big showy musical in many cities quite beyond what had been generally accepted as the prime market for such attractions was demonstrated. And it opened the door for others to follow.

Next on the list was *My Fair Lady*. Here was a real stunner— one of the great stage attractions of all time. It had everything— book, lyrics, score, and an outstanding acting company—all superbly costumed and directed. I was avid at the opportunity presented by this one and could not wait to get started. Terms were settled and I was engaged. After researching the records and laying out a tour that included returning to some cities as well as playing as many new cities as possible, I was suddenly dismissed and paid off. Someone in his own office had sold producer Herman Levin a bill of goods. Why not book the tour themselves and save the Olney fee? It would also avoid the arguments about allocation of playing time.

The net result was near disaster. Only a well-heeled show could have sustained the $120,000 loss attributed to this amateurishly booked tour which should have rather netted $100,000. The backers of the show probably never heard of this faux pas, having already been well rewarded for their investment.

No matter what the attraction, there are towns that are one-night stands and only one-night stands. For instance, a week was booked between Wichita Falls and San Angelo, Texas, that grossed less than $20,000, whereas the show needed $50,000. But, in originally laying out the tour, I was told time and again by producer Levin that I was wrong in only allocating one or two nights playing in places that would warrant at least a split week.

Other musical shows followed in ensuing years. One of the greatest was *The Sound of Music*. Not welcomed at the outset too enthusiastically by the New York press, the attraction, nevertheless, gained momentum with the general public that swept it forward to an acceptance seldom accorded to any similar attraction. The producer for the bus and truck company was Henry Guettel. He came up with not only an outstanding cast, headed by Jeannie Carson, but also an attractive production that was to gross $2,000,000 and repay a modest profit after returning the investment.

Even the lack of conventional facilities could not dim the impact of this beautiful production. At Florida State University in Tallahassee, *The Sound of Music* played in a gymnasium although the contract called for an "auditorium, well-lighted, heated," etc. Much of the physical production had to be left in the trucks, in spite of which the company received the most heart-warming ovation of the tour. Sometimes the cruder the accommodations, the more enthusiastic the audience. *Man of La Mancha,* for instance, was played on a temporary platform in the ballroom of Northern Illinois State University and was enthusiastically received.

Camelot, also produced by Guettel, was another standout and held up very well for two seasons. The Broadway production was built on the most lavish scale of any musical show up to that time. How the producer managed to give a similar effect with his bus and truck production and still get it into two forty-foot vans has always remained somewhat of a mystery.

For his next venture, Guettel was partnered with Arthur Cantor, and from then on his fortunes sagged. They contracted with Harold S. Prince to lease the rights and produce a touring version of *A Funny Thing Happened on the Way to the Forum.* And then, in turn, they contracted with National Performing Arts for a bus and truck tour. This tour was 80 percent booked when Prince decided it was not worth the trouble and canceled. I went directly to Prince in a desperate effort to salvage the tour. The only reasons offered for the cancellation were that they were apprehensive over the quality of the production, although they retained artistic approval and Guettal had demonstrated his ability previously. Also, they were being guaranteed a minimum royalty of $20,000 ($1,000 weekly for 20 weeks) which, on second thought, they deemed inadequate. Altogether it was a pretty flimsy pretext on which to cancel a show tour that was to have gone out on the road in another two months.

So, I was suddenly faced with a crisis, the only solution to which would be to find a suitable replacement show that would be acceptable to Broadway Theater Leagues and the other sponsors. An off-Broadway production of Rodgers and Hart's *The Boys from Syracuse* seemed to be the best answer. The rights were leased, financing arranged, and two producer–partners secured. They cast and produced an excellent company that was every bit as good as the Broadway show it replaced. But it was not always accepted by sponsors and, for the most part, turned out to be a box-office dud away from New York. Also, my partners in this venture turned out to be unreliable; and their financial statements were a mixture of fact and fiction. They were sued and ultimately went off to California leaving NPA to clean up the $42,000 loss.

There was one musical show in the mid 1960s that I wanted in the worst way. *How to Succeed in Business without Really Trying* was a natural for my expanding circuit. Meeting after meeting was held in an effort to arrive at a viable contract. I even took the unprecedented step of putting up a $10,000 advance to insure the contract. When it finally came through from the lawyers, however, there were so many ifs, ands, and buts and other stipulations added that could not be resolved that I gave up in disgust. The $10,000 was refunded and the tour dropped, although it had been confidently announced and booking had begun.

Later on a company manager booked this tour out of the producer's office. The resultant loss, of course, must be laid to management and not to the type of operation—it had already been proved successful.

Another major musical that did not materialize for NPA was *Fiddler on the Roof*. Having failed to deliver the *Forum*, as

227

promised, it was assumed by NPA that Harold Prince would make good at the next opportunity. After a year of fruitless conversation, the bus and truck company was turned over to another office, whose track record at that time was meager, indeed.

One of the most extraordinary musicals of this period was *Man of La Mancha*, which NPA toured for two seasons. The company was headed by David Atkinson as Don Quixote. The appearances in city after city were a successive round of ovations. Although *La Mancha* was a one-set show, nevertheless, it required a large cast and was not inexpensive to tour. The huge raked stage had to be carried in interlocking sections that filled a forty-foot van and required a large labor force to install.

It was a matter of principle with producers Albert W. Selden and Hal James to deliver a playing company with physical production and cast in every way comparable to the Broadway company. It was a genuine achievement, as well as a great satisfaction to be able to deliver such an attraction night after

Don Quixote, Sancho, and Dulcinea as caricatured by artist Al Hirschfeld.

night in city after city—sometimes as many as six cities in a single week. The tour was an immense credit to all concerned.

The huge success of Man of La Mancha was no accident but, rather, the result of several elements conspiring together to produce a rare achievement in the theater. To begin with, the attraction had a good book, developed by Dale Wasserman from a previous TV spectacular. To this was added an inimitable score by Mitch Leigh and the intriguing lyrics by Joe Darion. To make these elements jell was the task of director Albert Marre, who selected a superb cast. The results spoke for themselves: five years on Broadway and several national tours.

Not the least of the show's assets was the incomparable hit song, "The Impossible Dream" (it was originally titled "The Quest"). This is always an enormous asset in booking any road tour. In this particular case it was a plus to the same extent that The Sound of Music had a great album working for it ahead of the play dates on its tours, thus insuring record turnouts in city after city.

Another outstanding musical handled by NPA was Mame, derived from the original stage success Auntie Mame. Touring rights were acquired by Lee Guber and Shelley Gross. They took over the original road production and played out the prime time as well as the usual bus and truck cities. Taking over a heavy physical production may sound like a major economy at the outset, but it can be a detriment also. Starting out with four forty-foot trailer vans represented an enormous labor cost. Reduction of the show to two vans was soon accomplished by stage manager Irving Sudrow.

Nevertheless, the producers did not stint on the company itself. They provided an excellent cast that was handsomely costumed. And, for two seasons, the production represented a creditable achievement for the management.

Except for The Boys from Syracuse, all these musical shows had been booked for producers on an agency basis. In other words, NPA received a fixed commission on the producers' share of weekly receipts and was not involved in the casting and the other agonies of production. If the performances in any week were sold on flat fees, then the sum of these would constitute producers' share and be the basis on which royalties and commissions were settled.

Never anxious to become involved in production, nevertheless, I did so on those rare occasions when it became necessary in order to secure a certain attraction. The second musical I coproduced was *Canterbury Tales*, in which I was partnered with Hal James. I functioned as general manager and booker, and Hal cast and produced the show.

A man of taste in matters artistic, Hal found confinement within budgetary limitations a nuisance. He wound up with a top company only $4,500 over the weekly budget, which over the period of the tour constituted the deficit. Always affable and a long-time theater buff, Hal James's last production was at least an artistic triumph. And the production received high commendation in most of the cities played. Allen Whitehead, as consultant, was of inestimable aid in getting the production mounted.

Mention must be made of the artistic promotion literature of Gil Rich as well as the advance work on tour of Paul Anglim, press agent extraordinary. Their efforts seldom receive notice but are vital to successful presentations.

Our experience in handling and booking musical theater productions on tour brought a request from the management of the Metropolitan Opera Association to take on its new national company venture. For years this project had been under consideration as a means whereby to develop and train new talent for the senior company in New York and to provide a first-class troupe that would present opera on tour each season throughout America. It also would give talent experience and training. At the same time, many communities lacking this form of musical entertainment would be benefitted. The idea certainly had great merit and, with the vast resources of the Met, should have succeeded.

Accustomed as it was to offering grand opera on a lavish scale in its home base, the Met was unaccustomed to the exigencies of a bus and truck operation that necessarily had to function on a much more limited budget. The preparation of four productions, for instance, instead of two (as I had urged) required an additional expenditure of $250,000 at the outset, which could have been avoided. Two productions on tour would have been acceptable to sponsors, at least in the beginning.

After spending over a year working on plans and laying out ghost routes and making many local contacts, NPA was abruptly notified that the tour would be booked by the Sol Hurok office, a concert bureau. Although I had met with Anthony Bliss, president of the Metropolitan Opera Association, and had been substantially confirmed to handle and book the enterprise, this came as a big surprise, as well as a keen disappointment. To make the situation more palatable, at a meeting with Sol Hurok and officials of the Met, it was arranged that NPA would cooperate on the tour and receive "dollar-for-dollar" commissions commensurate with the compensation paid to Hurok. Nothing of the sort ever happened.

The Hurok booking of the tour was so inept that the Met itself had to take over and do some of the booking. Even then, there was at least one city in which the national company received no part of the receipts and reportedly ended up paying a portion of the local expenses. Even a one-man show could hardly survive under such circumstances. Unfortunately for the opera company and the musical public, a marvelous op-portunity was muffed and then had to be abandoned after two seasons. The loss reported in the press was $1,000,000. Under NPA direction the venture would have lost somewhat less than half that amount.

29

The Play's the Thing: Nonmusicals

> " 'Two trestles, four boards
> and a passion' are enough
> for a fine performance of a
> fine play."
> —Rosamond Gilder

Outside musical theater, the stage shows finding most public favor in these times are the comedies. And the epitome of most comedy writing is, of course, represented by the Neil Simon shows. Until recently these had been transposed from script to Broadway under the aegis of Saint Subber, for many years a leading Broadway producer. He has been most ably assisted in the pangs of the birth process by C. Edwin Knill, midwife and general manager extraordinary.

Barefoot in the Park was a real joy to tour. Depicting family situations that were cognizable to almost anyone, it was so spiced with humor throughout that the audiences were always in stitches. The next one was *The Odd Couple*, Simon's masterpiece. A smartly contrived comedy about two ex-husbands living together, it had structure, plot, more family situations, and a succession of brilliant comedy lines that kept the audiences in a continual state of uproar.

Never Too Late by Arthur Sumner Long was another very funny show shepherded to a deserved success on Broadway and on tour by Eddie Knill. The most was made of its one big joke, and the comedy was a huge success with the sponsors and their patrons.

Plaza Suite, another Neil Simon laugh riot, was a worthy addition to the touring comedy successes. Such attractions were a constant pleasure to handle season after season. They did not set out to deliver messages, nor did they deal directly with social and political problems of the day; rather, they were sheer entertainment–the first objective of good theater.

The other touring shows in which we took special satisfaction were the dramas, particularly the English shows. *The Royal Hunt of the Sun* was one of the great dramatic attractions of these times. Although it lost heavily on Broadway, this production was revamped by Theodore Mann for road travel and turned in a small profit from its tour. W.B. Brydon and Clayton Corbin were starred.

Although not rated a Broadway success in the usual terms, *Royal Hunt* continued to be highly spoken of for years after in complimentary terms by the sponsors. It was a unique and original concept of the Inca conquest by the Spanish conquistadores, rendered in striking dramatic terms that culminated in the stunning scene with the sunburst tower.

Two shows in this category were coproduced by National Performing Arts. *A Man for All Seasons* was courageously brought to Broadway by Robert Whitehead. He figured the show to be good for six weeks and hoped to break even on the venture. This show was first and foremost good theater. Not only was the Broadway engagement eminently successful—it ran for a full season—but the road tour was a real credit to all concerned. In partnership with Victor Samrock, we were proud of having sponsored the production. Robert Harris was imported from England to play Sir Thomas More. A sterling cast was assembled and polished off in final rehearsal by Bob Whitehead himself, thus assuring the artistic integrity of what proved to be a landmark up to that time. Eventually *A Man for All Seasons* was translated into a fabulous movie that was not only an achievement artistically but was reported to have made a lot of money.

The other coproduction was *Luther*, in which Joel Spector was general partner with National Performing Arts. Touring rights for this show, as well as the costumes and physical production, were acquired from David Merrick. Although it was a first-class dramatic offering, it proved difficult to book on the road. Efforts to secure a name performer proved fruitless, so a relatively unknown actor headed up the cast and was excellent. Months after the tour was settled out, a claim was received from the Merrick office for $5,000, based on some new interpretation of the royalty agreement. The tour almost, but not quite, paid out.

There were many other shows. Not to be overlooked is *You're A Good Man, Charlie Brown*, a charming compendium of scenes from the famed Charles Schulz cartoon strips, with a delightful musical setting. This was the first successful national tour ever made for an off-Broadway show, and the second for NPA. As indicated previously, *The Boys from Syracuse* had been booked nationally, but at a substantial loss.

The irrepressible Charlie Brown borne aloft by his adoring companions—Lucy, Linus, Schroeder, Patty and the ubiquitous Snoopy as drawn by the inimitable Charles M. Schulz.

During a thirty-two week tour, *Charlie Brown* was booked into 119 cities in the 1970–1971 season. So many requests were received that a second tour was arranged in the following season. The moving spirit in bringing out this attraction and developing its potentialities was an alert young producer, Gene Persson.

Fortunately for this show, star casting was never a problem. So many young performers were used in the several companies produced that a good cast could be assembled almost overnight. The public was interested mainly in seeing Charlie Brown, Snoopy, Lucy, and the other well-known characters in the flesh.

Casting for star names, however, has become more and more a serious problem each season. And the public always and forever wants stars. It would choose Ingrid Bergman in a bad play to a good play perfectly cast with unknowns and splendidly produced but lacking a single recognizable name. In retrospect, although only a few years have elapsed since the notable company of *Don Juan in Hell*, it has become almost impossible to entice star performers to tour. They either have a movie to make or their agents are dangling the lure of the next TV spectacle or even a bit part in a serial that may or may not come off. The TV commercials are now so lucrative that few can resist, though they tend to degrade the performer artistically.

Traveling conditions are really not all that bad. Performers are simply spoiled. One only has to read Lotta Crabtree's memoirs to realize what atrocious conditions she had to endure in order to reach her public a century ago. At the turn of the century, there were roughly three thousand one-night stands across the country, reached by all kinds of conveyances and under all kinds of unseasonable conditions. The reader should refer to chapter 18 for a reminder of the trouper spirit that animated Tyrone Power and stimulated him to tour across the country at a time when he was earning over one million dollars annually in films.

The tours for the Neil Simon shows always had to be booked lacking names of the cast. In the original Broadway companies there were usually "name" stars. Who could ever forget the inimitable performances of Walter Matthau and Art Carney in

The Odd Couple? Inspired casting for an inspired script plus the inspired directing of Mike Nichols made this production a complete standout. But bus and truck tours have to be booked a year ahead, and casts, especially stars, are not signed until two or three months ahead of rehearsal time. It is to the credit of Saint Subber, however, that he always eventually came up with acceptable stars for these road companies.

NPA, however, did not always have such luck. For *Shot in the Dark,* it was literally impossible to find a star that could be construed as a successor to Julie Harris. Herman Bernstein, general manager for producer Leland Hayward, had about given up when, out of the blue, a call came one day from Hollywood. Famed agent Irving Lazar was on the telephone, suggesting that Annie Fargé was ready and willing to play the lead—in fact, he said, she was made to order for the role of Josefa. Also, he continued, author Marcel Achard at one time had had her in mind when writing the play. Annie was hired.

It seems that Annie, for reasons never made clear, had been originally bypassed. But, then, she had no "name." She was right for the role of the pert peasant girl who got her noble lover involved. But Annie soon became a problem. Hardly had the tour gotten under way when she developed a prima donna complex. Stars of the prima donna variety are usually tolerable when they have attained a stature whereby public adulation and, therefore, box-office draw compels their employment. But who had ever even heard of Annie Fargé? Anyway, everyone lived through the tour. This was some years ago, and it would seem that Annie has yet to emerge as a major star.

On the other hand, there was the case of Patricia Smith—a lovely, sane, and talented young performer. During the extended Broadway run of *Mary, Mary,* she faithfully appeared night after night as understudy to the star, Barbara Bel Geddes. Certainly no one had ever heard of Pat Smith, but, after six months of fruitless looking, no "name" was ready to take on the assignment. So Pat was engaged for my tour and performed the role of Mary with distinction and eventually wound up in the number-one company on Broadway.

There was an advantage to having several companies on tour simultaneously. General managers are sometimes hesitant about putting more than one company on the road at the same time. If it's a big selling show, then the more the merrier. The various companies stimulate business for each other. Traveling expenses were reduced—certain companies can concentrate on certain areas instead of a single company trying to cover the whole country. When the late A.H. Woods came up with a hot success on Broadway, he would immediately put out as many companies as the traffic would bear. In one instance he had twelve companies on the road. The split-week tour for *Mary, Mary* was a record breaker—28,358 miles in forty-one weeks.

As well advertised as *Mary, Mary* was there was still confusion over the title. Letters of inquiry would come in about *Merry, Merry*; or *Merry Mary*; or *Marry, Marry*; or *Marry Mary*; etc. It is rare, indeed, for even the hit show to obtain national impact at once. Although it may have obtained smash success on Broadway overnight, it might be years obtaining the same recognition nationally.

It was during the last season of touring *Mary, Mary* that the motion picture was released while the NPA company was still on tour. Some local managers committed to play the show became panicky and were released from their contracts, with resultant losses to the company. Nevertheless, the picture came and went while the company was still on tour—it was a poor picture, but the stage company was first rate. And the public preferred the live company, in any event.

We had had a similar experience with *The Caine Mutiny Court Martial*. That picture (n.s.g. in *Variety* verbiage) came and went, and the tour continued. In the case of *The Music Man*, although producer Kermit Bloomgarden had control of the picture release, Warner Brothers was advertising its movie in some cities ahead of the touring company's play dates, until it was forced to desist.

Dorothy and I have always been among the most selective of presenters whether operating on a local, regional, or national level. Only a very small percentage of the attractions offered or available have we accepted for presentation. Some obviously commercial productions have been bypassed, usually because they were in bad taste or did not qualify as entertainment—the ultimate yardstick.

One of these was *Who's Afraid of Virginia Woolf?* although its booking would have meant $25,000 (more or less) in booking commissions. This show was well cast and well produced and became a critics' favorite. Having been urged to tour the show, I made the usual check with a few key sponsors, who were not encouraging. His own attitude was aptly put by Harold Jordan, for many years the able selector of cultural events for Indiana State University. Said Harold, in effect, "I know a family just like that represented in *Virginia Woolf.* I can't stand ten or fifteen minutes of such filthy talk, so why should I, or anyone else, spend four or five dollars to listen to such people for three hours?" Entertainment? A few of the Broadway Theater Leagues, however, insisted on booking the attraction, only to regret their decision later on.

Then there is the so-called theater of the absurd. Harold Pinter's *Homecoming* had a fair run on Broadway in the season 1966–1967. They must have come out of sheer curiosity (egged on by the critics, some of whose penchant for the oddball only too often leads the customers astray), or perhaps it was the shock value of the piece that intrigued their attendance. One explanation given was that it was intended to show "human emotions in reverse." But why should talent be squandered on such nonsense?

The theater has fortunately survived other passing fads, e.g., the theater of cruelty; the theater of fact; the theater of improvisation; the theater of social change; and, more recently, the theater of filth. William Shakespeare, and even Bernard Shaw — and perhaps Neil Simon — will still emerge as the epitome of good writing and, hence, good theater. And works by writers such as these will continue to be produced long after the faddists have been forgotten.

30

Art Versus Industry

> *"The producer's job is to
> translate moods and supply
> the medium by which they
> are transmitted to
> audiences."*
> —David Belasco

Although the advent of the motion picture, followed by the invasion of radio and finally by the overwhelming spread of television, may have greatly altered the general character of the presentations business, it has not dispensed entirely with the thrill and the excitement that are part of live stage attractions. The latest prediction in the amusement trade papers is that showmen will shortly be eliminated. They will be replaced by research, statistics, ratings, and the other adjuncts by which big business operates to ascertain its selling power and profitable operation.

Does this imply that heart and inspiration are no longer to be motivating factors in show business? Does this imply that the transmutation of the presentations business has finally run full circle? Once an art, has it now joined the ranks of industry and become big business instead?

Not necessarily! The public will always dress up to go out for a gala evening and pay well to see exciting live entertainment presented   provided the circumstances are such as to intrigue its fancy and thereby invite the necessary expense and effort.

Half a century ago there were talented giants behind the presentation of stage art. When we refer to the legitimate stage, there were Charles and Daniel Frohman, Florenz Ziegfeld, David Belasco, Henry Miller, John Golden, Klaw and Erlanger, Arthur Hopkins, Charles Dillingham, and others.

In opera, Gatti-Casazza, the great impresario of the Metropolitan Opera Company, could command such talents as Toscanini, the de Reszkes, Caruso, Ponselle, Chaliapin, Bori, Farrar, Sembrich, Nordica, Martinelli, Eames, and many others.

In concert, there was a galaxy of big-name artists: Josef Hofmann, Rachmaninoff, Paderewski, Kreisler, Schumann-Heink, the Damrosches, John McCormack, Galli-Curci, Caruso, Toscanini, Koussevitzky, and others.

Then along came Sergei Diaghilev, who was to pioneer the successful presentation of still another form of stage art: ballet. Sol Hurok was to carry on in developing a special public, the balletomanes, who would confirm the right of ballet to recognition as a stage art for its own sake.

At the turn of the century there were something like three thousand legitimate theaters across the country. Stock companies were numerous, and one-night stands for traveling shows were the rule rather than the exception. And there were many traveling opera troupes geared to the one-nighters. Today, the potential profitable stops for such companies have shrunk to a mere fraction, possibly around 10 percent. As a result, there are ordinarily less than two dozen professional touring shows traveling on the road at any one time; the ranks of professional concert managers have thinned to a mere handful; and impresarios in the tradition are scarcely to be found at all.

The wellsprings of creative effort in the theater are still found in the off-Broadway situations and similar enterprising entrepreneurs in the Hollywood area. From time to time, the tributary or regional theater blossoms forth with worthwhile artistic offerings.

Originally weaned from live stage presentations by movies, then lured by the siren voice of radio, the public's taste for mass entertainment was finally taken over by television. In the wake of these contrivancies, there has arisen another giant industry concerned with the mechanics of bringing news, soap operas, quiz programs, vaudeville, and many other forms of so-called entertainment into individual homes.

In the meantime, what has happened to drama, opera, ballet, and concert presentations? Fortunately, these basic arts of stage entertainment have not yet been taken over by the mechanicians. In spite of efforts to conform such class attractions to mediocrity, they are still lusty and thriving. And, it is safe to say, they will withstand the assaults and maintain their integrity as distinctive art forms.

What can ever be comparable to an evening in the theater, watching the Royal Ballet Company perform *The Sleeping Beauty*; or brilliant musical productions such as *South Pacific*, or *My Fair Lady*, or *Man of La Mancha* unfold on stage; the four stars of *Don Juan in Hell* parry the wit of Bernard Shaw; the notable figure of Paderewski or Kreisler performing his own compositions; or attending an evening in the concert hall with Eugene Ormandy and the superb Philadelphia Orchestra? And there have been many other similarly inspired evenings within the memories of our time. Such will always command our attention — and attendance in person as well.

There are certain moments in stellar performances that will always remain standouts. Who could ever forget the Don Cossack Male Chorus rendering the "Song of the Volga Boatmen," or Paul Robeson singing "Water Boy" and "Old Man River," or Rachmaninoff playing his own Prelude in C-sharp minor, or Marian Anderson's singing of "Ave Maria," or Lauritz Melchior's lusty "Viva La Compagnie"?

The hucksters with the moneybags, however, are now in the saddle as purveyors of mass entertainment. Perhaps most talent could never hope for more than nominal recognition. To these the new mechanical mediums have come as a genuine windfall. Many of them are now reaping earnings beyond their fondest dreams. But some of the smart talent is preserving its value by not making itself too common, by being seen or heard only on occasion and at a price.

The subversion of the stage arts, whereby the entire field of entertainment could be said to have become an adjunct of the general ballyhoo to whip up commodity sales fortunately has not yet come to pass. Unfortunately, the money has proved too strong a lure for some of the name stage talent to resist, even though they are not that hard up.

It can be hoped that the prostitution of stage talent in the interests of commercial advertising already has been carried quite far enough. Of course, there was some precedent in times past when sundry talents were engaged as a lure for the peddlers of snake oil and a variety of patent medicines.

Dorothy and I had to conform our operation to suit the changing times. Independent managers and producers for twenty years, we were ready to discontinue our concert bureau when it became outmoded, in order to enter a newer type of presentations operation in association with Charles Laughton and Paul Gregory. Progressing from local through a regional operation to management on a national scale, finally we came into control of a national theater circuit that numbered ninety-two cities coast to coast.

Today the producer is reduced to comparative impotence, particularly in the mechanical media, when one considers his former commanding position in the presentations business. In the handling of live stage attractions, however, he still retains some authority. At least he has the free choice of script and director, and, generally, of the performers. His efforts, however, are hemmed about by a varied assortment of unions more bent than ever on regulation to the nth degree, and their greed seems to have no limits. Certainly they have blunted more production activity, thereby contributing to the reduction of shows appearing on Broadway.

Stage arts blossom and thrive in a free and unfettered atmosphere. If labor unions were not so self-centered, they would encourage the creative aspects of the stage arts and thus join producers and managers in a cooperative effort that would be of more long-run benefit to all concerned. In the mass entertainment media, of course, unions have a function, just as they always have had in mass industry. Under the stress of present-day conditions the producer of stage attractions is only too often congratulating himself on breaking even.

In the Louisville *Times* of October 21, 1960, Sherwood Kohn wrote,

> The American theatre's most pressing problem, beyond that of finding first-rate material, is that of its ever-burgeoning overhead. The costs of mounting even the simplest production have gotten completely out of hand, and with them has gone the price of tickets.
>
> The problem, like most financial dilemmas today, has become a two-edged sword, balking small producers on the one hand, frustrating the average theatregoer on the other. But there is hope rising in the hinterlands, where the squeeze is not so painful.

A word here about facilities: the company on any extended tour by bus and truck must be prepared to play under any and all sorts of conditions. These will include gymnasiums with or without a temporary platform at one end; movie theaters with stages reconverted to again accommodate stage shows; all kinds of auditoriums with or without rigging; stages too shallow to take the production, so that the apron has to be built out; stages with solid side and rear walls, such as to preclude exits and entrances and hanging even a cyclorama; acoustics of varying quality, so that a show must carry its own system to insure good projection; dressing rooms with or without hot or cold running water, or both; sometimes no dressing rooms at all, so that classrooms or other temporary facilities have to be used, etc. etc.

A facility that was too uncivilized brought an immediate outcry of anguish from Ellsworth Wright, watchdog on behalf of the Actors' Equity Association for the rights and creature comforts of the members. He was usually inclined to a measure of tolerance, but glaring deficiencies had to be corrected or members of Equity did not play that facility the next time around.

The previous recital must not be taken to negate the fact that many colleges and universities, as well as some cities, have been erecting new auditoriums and theaters that are the last word in comfort and equipment. Perhaps the model facilities for stage presentations are to be found in Canada, where the provincial and national authorities have taken a much more than casual interest in providing the best all-around accommodations for the performing arts. These modern facilities are to be found clear across the country from Vancouver to Montreal.

The first new Broadway theaters in over forty years are housed in office buildings. And so the commercial theater becomes even more commercial. Of course, most Broadway theaters are undistinguished anyway. The one that did have an aspect of theatricality was the Ziegfeld Theater (designed by Josef Urban), and that was torn down in 1969.

On the other hand, new facilities have been going up all over the country. Altogether they represent a great variety of tastes and competence, with usually a deficiency here and there. Occasionally a facility emerges that is right in every department and from every standpoint. Certainly the availability of new facilities for the presentation of concerts, ballet, and stage shows are a sign of the times; a bright and shining beacon that should encourage and stimulate interest in the performing arts throughout the country.

It is here, beyond Broadway, in the country at large, that theater is more and more realizing greater satisfaction; and seasonal grosses are now rivaling those on Broadway. And the pressures and drawbacks and costs of Broadway production are mostly lacking elsewhere.

On the other hand, the manager or producer in the mechanical media of entertainment is not what the label implies. He is, rather, the harried go-between pushed hither and yon by the sponsor (who pays the bills), the network, and the technicians. Finally, he is forced to conform to a frustrating array of union regulations. Their business agents and lawyers must have worked many long hours overtime to have devised so many expensive traps for the hapless producer. When the show is in rehearsal, the producer counts for very little. The technicians take over, and he soon learns what he can and cannot do. Then, if the show flops, he gets the blame. If it achieves any measure of success, then the bouquets go to the performers.

As television becomes more settled in its ways and motion pictures become adjusted to the new order, it may well be that the lines will be roughly drawn somewhere between class and mass entertainment. To defray the enormous bills of the latter, the production staff has to cater to taste as revealed in the mysterious ratings, all for the sake of the commercial label attached. Except in the interests of sheer philanthropy, industry is obviously not going to stand the cost of too much experimentation. It wants to create buying demand by tried-and-true methods.

Genuine creative effort, therefore, must continue to seek its outlet through live performances. And, under the new order, its monetary reward should be at least ample, if not found climbing into "the point of no return" taxwise.

Just as long as the basic art forms of stage entertainment retain some measure of popular favor, there will continue a need for the intrepid producer. There will always be inspired leaders in any field; but in our case, they will continue to find their greatest degree of freedom in expression on the legitimate stage.

Good drama or good music, and by these terms we mean live on-stage shows and live on stage concerts, can originate anywhere. No institution, or city, or country, has an "in" on talent. And the sun does not rise and set on Broadway. Inspiration, creativity, and talent can originate at any moment anywhere. Today they are more than likely to be found *beyond* Broadway—unfettered and undeterred by union greed and the inordinate expenses that are chilling the Broadway theater.

Fortunately, for the theater's own well-being and to insure continuity in the performing arts, there are now over a hundred colleges and universities conferring theater degrees. Also, there is a noticeable upsurge in the activities of the regional theaters, of which there are now more than thirty worthwhile operations to be counted. So, to future audiences we say: Look to those sources *beyond* Broadway that are today contributing so much to good theater for your entertainment.

*"All the world's a stage and
all the men and women merely players:
They have their entrances and their exits,
and one man in his time plays many parts."*
—*Shakespeare*

Appendices

(including Roster of Olney Presentations)

247

Daggett Lee
New Haven, Connecticut

Mrs. Archer Linde,
Phoenix, Arizona

Marvin McDonald
Atlanta, Georgia

Michaux Moody
Richmond, Virginia

William A. Mortensen
Hartford, Connecticut

I. L. Myers
Memphis, Tennessee

Arthur Oberfelder
Denver, Colorado

Mr. and Mrs. Julian Olney
White Plains, New York

Mr. and Mrs. D. G. Price
San Diego, California

Aaron Richmond
Boston, Massachusetts

Mrs. Edna W. Saunders
Houston, Texas

Arthur M. See
Rochester, New York

Charles A. Sink
Ann Arbor, Michigan

J. H. Thuman
Cincinnati, Ohio

A. Tremblay
Ottawa, Canada

C. W. Van Lopik
Detroit, Michigan

Elmer Wilson
Pasadena, California

Harry Zelzer
Chicago, Illinois

CONCERT ATTRACTIONS
(presented during 1931–1953)

American Ballet

Marian Anderson

Salvatore Baccaloni

Bali and Java Dancers

Ballet Russe de Monte Carlo

The Ballet Theater

Simon Barer

Ethel Bartlett and Rae
  Robertson

Harry Belafonte

Lucretia Bori

Boston Symphony Orchestra
  Leonard Bernstein, conductor

Alexander Brailowsky

Robert Casadesus

Feodor Chaliapin

Cleveland Orchestra
  Artur Rodzinski, conductor

Don Cossack Chorus

Richard Crooks

Nelson Eddy

Mischa Elman

Georges Enesco

Angna Enters

Vicente Escudero

First Piano Quartet

Kirsten Flagstad

Raya Garbousova

Percy Grainger

Jascha Heifetz

Myra Hess

Josef Hofmann

Vladimir Horowitz

Iglesias Ballet Español

José Iturbi

Jooss Ballet

Fritz Kreisler

Lotte Lehmann

Oscar Levant

Little Orchestra Society

Luboshutz and Nemenoff

Jeanette McDonald

Mantovani and Orchestra

Nino Martini

Lauritz Melchior

James Melton

Yehudi Menuhin

Robert Merrill and Orchestra

Metropolitan Quartet —
  Rose Bampton, Edward
  Johnson, Grace Moore,
  Richard Bonelli

Nathan Milstein

Patrice Munsel

National Symphony Orchestra
  Hans Kindler, conductor

New York Philharmonic
  Orchestra
  Leopold Stokowski,
  conductor

Sigrid Onegin

Jan Peerce

Philadelphia Orchestra
  Eugene Ormandy, conductor

Gregor Piatigorsky

Lily Pons

Rosa Ponselle

Sergei Rachmaninoff

Paul Robeson and Hall Johnson
  Choir

Rochester Symphony Orchestra
  José Iturbi, conductor
  Stephen Hero, soloist

Artur Rubinstein

Sadlers Wells Ballet

Ruth St. Denis and Dancers

Shan Kar and Dancers

Robert Shaw Chorale

Ted Shawn and Dancers

Mia Slavenska and Dancers

Solomon

Albert Spalding

Eleanor Steber

Giuseppe di Stefano

Isaac Stern

Feruccio Tagliavini

· Alec Templeton

John Charles Thomas

Lawrence Tibbett

Tamara Toumanova

Vienna Boys' Choir

Vronsky and Babin

Ethel Waters and Hall Johnson
  Choir

Ljuba Welitch

Roger Williams

Efrem Zimbalist

RIDGEWAY THEATER PRODUCTIONS
(Seasons 1939 to 1942)

Tallulah Bankhead in *The Second Mrs. Tanqueray*, by Sir Arthur Wing Pinero

Tallulah Bankhead in *Her Cardboard Lover*, by Jacques Deval and P. G. Wodehouse

Diana Barrymore in *Captain Jinks of the Horse Marines*, by Clyde Fitch

Ethel Barrymore in *Whiteoaks*, by Maso de la Roche

Ethel Barrymore in *The Constant Wife*, by Somerset Maugham

Ethel Barrymore in *The School for Scandal*, by Oliver Goldsmith

Ethel Barrymore in *The Corn Is Green*, by Emlyn Williams

Mary Boland in *Meet the Wife*, by Lyn Sterling

Romney Brent and Gina Malo in *The World Walks In*, by John Golden

Kitty Carlisle in *Tonight or Never*, by Lili Hatvany

Ruth Chatterton in *Tomorrow and Tomorrow*, by Philip Barry

Mady Christians in *Watch on the Rhine*, by Lillian Hellman

Peggy Conklin in *The Perfect Alibi*, by A. A. Milne

Gladys Cooper and Philip Merivale in *Spring Meeting*, by M. J. Farrell

Jane Cowl in *Easy Virtue*, by Noel Coward

Frank Craven in *Village Green*, by Carl Allensworth

Eddie Dowling in *George Washington Slept Here*, by George S. Kaufman and Moss Hart

Gracie Fields in *Fun for All*, a musical revue

Bramwell Fletcher in *Petrified Forest*, by Robert E. Sherwood

Grace George in *Kind Lady*, by Edward Chodorov

Ruth Gordon in *Here Today*, by George Oppenheimer

Paul and Grace Hartman in *Tonight at Eight-Thirty*, by Noel Coward

Paul and Grace Hartman in *Two for the Show*, a musical revue

Paul and Grace Hartman in *Mr. and Mrs. North*, by Owen Roberts

Paul and Grace Hartman in *Keep 'Em Happy*, a musical revue

Miriam Hopkins in *The Guardsman*, by Ferenc Molnar

Edward Everett Horton in *Springtime for Henry*, by Benn Levy

Buster Keaton in *The Gorilla*, by Ralph Spence

Jessie Royce Landis in *Twelve Midnight*, by Frank W. Delmar and Harry Wagstaff Gribble

251

Francis Lederer in *No Time for Comedy*, by S.N. Behrman

Beth Merrill and Brandon Peters in *The Two Mrs. Carrolls*, by Martin Vale

Mary Morris and Edith Atwater in *Fashion*, by Anna Cora Mowatt

Conrad Nagel in *The Male Animal*, by James Thurber

Elizabeth Patterson and William and Nedda Harrigan in *The Rich Get Richer*, by Mary Hall

Tom Powers in *Goodbye Again*, by George Haight and Allen Scott

Tom Powers in *Second Man*, by S.N. Behrman

Joan Roberts in *Heels Together*, by Harlan Thompson

Paul Robeson in *The Emperor Jones*, by Eugene O'Neill

Sir C. Aubrey Smith in *Old English*, by John Galsworthy

Ezra Stone in *What a Life*, by Clifford Goldsmith

Gloria Swanson in *Reflected Glory*, by George Kelly

June Walker in *The Late Christopher Bean*, by Sidney Howard

Ruth Weston and Edith King in *On the House*, by Ivor Novello

Gene Kelly, Hiram Sherman, Ruth Mata and Eugene Hari, Bill Johnson, and Pat Harrington in *Two Weeks with Pay*, by Ted Fetter and Dick Lewine

252

NATIONAL TOURS FOR BROADWAY PLAYS
1960 to 1970
(4,259 Nights in 317 Cities by Bus and Truck)

Barefoot in the Park

The Best Man

The Boys from Syracuse

Butterflies Are Free

Camelot

Canterbury Tales

Carnival

Critics Choice

Last of the Red Hot Lovers

Luther

Mame

A Man for All Seasons

Man of La Mancha

Mary, Mary

The Music Man

Never Too Late

The Odd Couple

Plaza Suite

Royal Hunt of the Sun

A Shot in the Dark

The Sound of Music

A Thousand Clowns

You're a Good Man,
Charlie Brown

NATIONAL TOURS FOR
LAUGHTON–GREGORY SHOWS

Don Juan in Hell, by Bernard Shaw and starring Charles Boyer, Sir Cedric Hardwicke, Agnes Moorehead, and Charles Laughton

John Brown's Body, by Stephen Vincent Benét and starring Tyrone Power, Judith Anderson, and Raymond Massey

The Caine Mutiny Court Martial, by Herman Wouk and starring Henry Fonda, John Hodiak, and Lloyd Nolan

The Rivalry, by Norman Corwin and starring Martin Gabel, Agnes Moorehead, and Raymond Massey

Three for Tonight, a musical revue, starring Harry Belafonte, Marge and Gower Champion, and the Voices of Walter Schumann

NATIONAL TOURS FOR SPECIAL PRODUCTIONS

Fujiwara Opera Company of Japan in *Madame Butterfly* and *The Mikado*

Back to Methuselah, by Bernard Shaw and starring Tyrone Power, Faye Emerson, and Arthur Treacher

The World of Carl Sandburg, by Norman Corwin and starring Bette Davis and Gary Merrill

Sigmund Romberg and Orchestra, with Marie Nash, soloist

Lauritz Melchior and Orchestra, with Otto Seyfert, conductor

Hollywood Bowl Production of *Gay Nineties Night* starring Patricia Morrison

Canterbury Tales – Broadway Musical starring Martyn Green

LECTURES AND SOLO PERFORMANCES

Jack Aranson in *Moby Dick* by Herman Melville

Admiral Richard E. Byrd: "Conquering the Antarctic"

Rt. Hon. Winston Churchill: "The World Crisis"

Ruth Draper: Monologues

Maurice Evans: Readings from Shakespeare

Burton Holmes: Travelogues

Martin and Osa Johnson: "Wonders of the Congo" and "Wings Over Africa"

Elsa Lanchester: Monologues

Charles Laughton: Readings from the Bible, Dickens, and Shakespeare

Agnes Moorehead: *Sorry, Wrong Number* and readings

Dorothy McGrayne Olney: "Highlights of Drama"

Eleanor Roosevelt: "The Importance of Memorial Day"

Cornelia Otis Skinner: Monologues

Tamara Toumanova – Dancer

MISCELLANEOUS ATTRACTIONS

Connecticut Opera Company in *La Boheme* and *La Traviata*

San Carlo Grand Opera Company in *Faust*, with Leon Rothier

New York Opera Comique in *The Chocolate Soldier*

Greek Evans Company in *The Geisha* and *Robin Hood*

Hurok Production of *Die Fledermaus*, with Irra Pettina

Theatre Guild's *Oklahoma*

Adrienne Morrison's Children's Players

Tony Sarg's Marionettes in *Pinocchio*

Salzburg Marionettes in Mozart's *The Magic Flute*

Margaret Webster's Shakespeare Company in *Hamlet* and *MacBeth*

Bernard Shaw's G. B. *eSsence of Women*, with Violet Heming

Fred Waring and his Pennsylvanians

Spike Jones and his *Musical Depreciation Revue*

Stan Kenton and his Orchestra

Duke Ellington and his Orchestra

EVENTS MANAGED

Westchester Music Festival, Hugh Ross, music director; featuring
Philadelphia Orchestra, Eugene Ormandy, conducting

United States Marine Band in Joint Concert with Gracie Fields

Charles Ives Centennial Concert, featuring Leonard Bernstein, conducting the American Symphony Orchestra; McHenry Boatwright, soloist

Pro Tennis with Jack Kramer, Pancho Segura, Bobby Riggs, and Pancho Gonzales